visits with the

⋙ Amish ⋘

visits with the

⋑ Amish ⋐

impressions of the plain life

Linda Egenes

with woodcuts by Mary Azarian

Iowa State University Press
Ames, Iowa

Linda Egenes has written about the Amish for *Cobblestone, Plain, The Iowa Source,* and *The Plain Reader.* She is the author of several books and recently completed a children's novel set in the Amish community of Kalona, Iowa. Egenes teaches literary journalism at Maharishi University of Management in Fairfield, Iowa. She holds degrees in elementary education and professional writing.

Mary Azarian is a Vermont artist, award-winning illustrator of books, full-time printmaker, and founder of Farmhouse Press. She won the Caldecott medal in 1998 for illustrating *Snowflake Bentley.* Her book, *The Farmer's Alphabet,* was nominated for an American Book Award.

© 2000 Iowa State University Press
All rights reserved

Designed by Justin Eccles

Iowa State University Press
2121 South State Avenue, Ames, Iowa 50014

Orders: 1-800-862-6657
Office: 1-515-292-0140
Fax: 1-515-292-3348
Web site: www.isupress.edu

The names of many people in the book have been changed to protect their privacy.

Woodcuts by Mary Azarian. Used by permission.
Figure 1. From "Buckles, Snaps and Straps," *Plain,* No. 10, December 1995, p. 22. Used by permission.
Figure 2. Illustration by Jo Ann M. Gesner.
Portions of Chapter 1 were adapted from the article "A Day With the Amish" from COBBLE-STONE's November 1987 issue: The Amish, © 1987, Cobblestone Publishing Company, 30 Grove Street, Suite C, Peterborough, NH 03458. Reprinted by permission of the publisher.
Portions of Chapters 2-10 previously appeared in *Plain* published by The Center of Plain Living, 60805 Pigeon Dr., Barnesville, OH.
Excerpts from *The Budget* reprinted by permission of Sugarcreek Budget Publishers, Sugarcreek, OH.
Drakesville Amish School song lyrics by Lena (Mast) Yoder.

∞ Printed on acid-free paper in the United States of America

First edition, 2000

International Standard Book Number: 0-8138-2609-8

CIP information is available.

The last digit is the print number: 9 8 7 6 5 4 3 2 1

For my parents,
who, like the Amish,
passed on a solid
sense of values
to their children

contents

preface

I was driving down a gravel road near Kalona, Iowa, looking for Norman Kauffman, an Amish man who had agreed to talk to me. When I stopped by his farmhouse, his wife directed me to their neighbor's field. Norman was putting up corn silage with his silage ring, a group of neighbors who shared labor and machinery during harvest season the same way old-time farmers throughout America used to do.

I passed a group of Amish children walking home from school, the girls swinging their lunch buckets, peeking shyly from their black bonnets and long dark capes. The boys ducked under a fence, taking a shortcut through a pasture, their straw hats bobbing as they dashed across the grass.

It was late afternoon in fall, when the sky seems more blue, the sunlight more golden, and the air more crisp and exhilarating. Hoping to find Norman, I stopped my car by a group of Amish farmers pitching cornstalks onto a wagon. Something about the scene—sun slanting golden on the corn, beards and hats bowing as men gathered cornstalks by hand, giant russet-coated work horses swishing creamy tails—created a feeling of euphoria. I felt as if I had entered a time warp, suddenly finding myself transported to an earlier century. In 13 years of visiting the Amish, I often experienced this feeling of timelessness.

Somehow, I found, when freed of the telephone ring, television prattle, and superhighway roar, my head cleared. On my visits I felt light and unfettered, and extraneous thoughts evaporated. Surely there was some kind of enchantment to be found in the plain life of the Amish.

Anyone who sees an Amish covered buggy lumbering along as cars whiz by can't help but wonder about the people hidden inside. What would it be like to grow up without a car, without TV, without a telephone? What would it be like to finish school in eighth grade? These were a few of the questions I set out to answer for myself and for my readers.

Having grown up in suburbia, I have always been fascinated by cultures that reflect a more traditional lifestyle outside the grip of America's consumer-driven society. As a member of a spiritually oriented community myself, I did not seek out the Amish for answers to life's deeper questions. Rather, I sought them out in appreciation. Appreciation for their ability to put their Christian ideals into practice, their ability to reject television and other influences that they find harmful to family and community life, their willingness to pursue a lifestyle that preserves their values even if it is totally at odds with modern society. I was attracted to their slower pace of life and to their open, trusting faces.

I learned many things while researching this book. I learned that the Amish work hard to maintain their way of life, and they are willing to sacrifice much to attain that goal. I also learned that the Amish do not appear burdened by their work. Because they wear dark, plain colors and old-fashioned clothes, I expected to find a somber, humorless people. In contrast to this solemn and formal public image, I found instead that a lively sense of humor, gentle teasing, and frequent joking were common.

Of course, each community has a mix of different personalities, just like anywhere in the world. But because they do not depend on television or other forms of electronic entertainment, I think the Amish enjoy visiting, singing, and laughing together more than others.

The stories in this book are my impressions of Amish family life as I experienced them. They do not in any way attempt to represent all Amish people or families. Yet these are true stories about real people.

Despite the fact that they live in a closed society, the seven Amish families described in this book warmly welcomed me into their homes. They spent time reviewing each story to make sure that even small details were accurate before it was published. I am grateful for their friendship and their willingness to share these stories of Amish family life.

I'd like to thank all of the Amish families who opened their homes and hearts to me. Without their help and encouragement, this book would never have happened. There are so many others to whom I feel grateful. Dr. Jim Karpen and Dr. Steven Schneider taught me how to write simple and clear nonfiction. Scott Savage published these articles in *Plain* and never let me stray from my true vision. Claudia Petrick at *The Iowa Source* gave me a start by publishing my first articles on the Amish. Mary Zeilbeck, my dear friend and writing buddy, helped me market the stories outside of Iowa. My critique group—Janet Adelson, Caree Connet, and Cheryl Johnson—have provided a steady supply of moral support and insightful feedback for many years. Faithful friends Linda Brittingham, Katherine Doak, Maryanne Falk, Charlotte Judge, Katie Smith, and Cora Taylor kept me company on out-of-town trips. Victoria Shoemaker at The Speller Agency/West so generously contributed her help and guidance. And thanks to David Luthy, David Garber, Ervin Gingerich, and Katie Yoder, who spent many hours helping me find answers to difficult questions.

I feel grateful to Janet Hronek, Kathy Walker, and Sherry Johnson at Iowa State University Press, all of whom appreciated the spirit of Amish life and understood my intentions perfectly. Carla Tollefson patiently and skillfully made sure my words said what I really meant.

Most of all I'd like to thank my husband, Tom, who inspired me to start writing and encouraged me to keep going.

introduction: *who are the Amish?*

Children reciting their lessons in a one-room country school. ... A row of black buggies parked in a hayfield beside a highway. ... Two grandmothers in black bonnets and capes conversing in German at a country store. ... A group of women and young girls clustered around a quilting frame, sewing tiny, painstaking stitches on a colorful design. ... A young man and his girl driving home from a Sunday "singing" in an open buggy on a moonlit night.

They call themselves the Plain People. The men and women known as the Old Order Amish till their fields with horse and plow, travel by horse and buggy, and live without electricity or telephones.

Today the Amish are thriving. Their population has more than doubled during the last 25 years. There are now over 144,000 Amish people scattered in communities throughout North America, and their numbers continue to grow.

origins of the Amish in the United States and Iowa

The Amish originally came to America in search of religious freedom, fleeing severe persecution in Germany, Switzerland, and Alsace (an area of France bordering Germany and Switzerland in which a German dialect is spoken). The first Amish families arrived in 1737 and settled in Lancaster County, Pennsylvania.

Another wave of immigration followed between 1815 and 1860, and the Amish eventually spread to 20 other states, including Iowa. Today no Amish groups remain in Europe.

The Amish were among the first settlers to arrive in Iowa. In 1846 three Amish families from Ohio settled in the Kalona area, and this flourishing community of 800 is now the largest Amish group west of the Mississippi. In 1914 a small group who felt that the Kalona community had become too worldly migrated north to Buchanan County, near Hazelton, and established a community, now estimated at 400, that is the second largest Old Order Amish settlement in the state.

Today there are three other Amish communities in Iowa: the Milton-Pulaski settlement in southeastern Iowa, formed in 1968; the Bloomfield-Drakesville community south of Ottumwa, formed in 1971; and the Riceville-McIntire settlement in northern Iowa, started by six families in 1975.

religious beliefs

The Amish faith originated in the Swiss Anabaptist movement, which was started by reformers dissatisfied with the Reformation. The name "Amish" was given to followers of Jacob Amman, an Anabaptist minister in Alsace, France, who advocated stricter reforms and broke away from other Anabaptists in 1693.

The Amish, like other Anabaptists such as the Mennonites and Hutterites, do not believe in baptizing their children at birth. Rather, they wait until late adolescence, when the young person can consciously choose the responsibility of life in the church.

The vows taken at baptism, usually from ages 16 to 18, follow six to eight meetings of religious instruction. The young person solemnly vows to follow the rules of the church and community until death.

Using the life of Christ and the Sermon on the Mount as models, the Amish feel it should be possible to live Christian ideals in everyday life. The Amish believe in family and community unity, brotherly love, separation from the world, humility, nonviolence, and peacefulness.

The Amish are taught to greet any verbal or bodily assault with silence, and they take literally the Bible teaching to "turn the other cheek." Even if others attack them (which unfortunately happens in some communities when non-Amish teenagers harass them), the Amish will turn away without responding. Because of their firm belief in nonviolence, they will not serve in the armed forces. For this reason many Amish men were imprisoned and treated badly during World War II.

Because of their religious beliefs, the Amish do not vote in elections, participate in government, or sue others in lawsuits even if they have been wronged.

The Old Order Amish do not believe in missionary activity or persuading others to join their faith. While they aspire to "be a light unto the world" and are exhorted to provide an example to Amish youth through their actions, they do not expect or even desire outsiders to join them. Although highly disciplined in exercising their own faith, they accept non-Amish people as they are.

The Amish emphasize obedience to the word of God, which includes obedience to the rules of the church, elders, and parents. To obey the rules of the church and community is to have hope of salvation, which the Amish believe is not ensured until the judgment day after death.

rules of conduct

The Amish follow the same customs that they did 500 years ago, with few changes. They still speak a German dialect called "Pennsylvania German" at home (a language mistakenly known by many Americans as "Pennsylvania Dutch," Dutch being a corrupted pronunciation of *Deutsch*, which means German). They learn English at school, and they refer to non-Amish people as "The English."

A large part of Amish faith involves following the rules and regulations of church and community life. From an early age, the Amish learn to follow the *Ordnung*, a strict body of rules that govern behavior, dress, and attitude. In order to shun "the ways of the world," the Amish reject modern technology (such as cars, telephones, television, and electricity) and dress in a way that sets them apart.

A man's jacket, for instance, will not have buttons or lapels.

The Amish are called "hook-and-eyers" because for the most part they use hooks and eyes for fastening their clothing rather than buttons or zippers. (The exception is men's work shirts, which usually feature buttons for safety's sake.) Amish men do not wear mustaches but wear untrimmed beards after marriage. These particular customs date back to the time when the Amish were persecuted by the Swiss Army, in which the soldiers wore buttons, lapels, and mustaches but not beards. Men's and boys' clothing includes suspenders, broadfall pants, and wide-brimmed hats.

The Amish believe the Ordnung brings them closer to God. For instance, Amish women and girls do not ever cut their hair. They braid it and hide it modestly under a lightweight white or black organdy prayer cap while indoors. When in public outdoors, they wear black wool bonnets that are similar to those worn by pioneer women over a century ago. These practices are in accord with Bible verses which instruct women to cover their heads when worshiping, and since a woman could close her eyes in prayer at any moment of the day, she must always be prepared.

In accord with other scriptural injunctions, women do not use makeup and they wear modest, long dresses covered with aprons and fastened with straight pins instead of buttons. The fabrics must be plain, not patterned.

differences between communities

The Ordnung may differ slightly in different communities. For instance, among the Amish in Kalona, Iowa, where farms are larger than in the eastern United States, gasoline-powered tractors for plowing the fields are used as long as the tires are steel-rimmed instead of air-filled (pneumatic) rubber tires. That same community does not use automatic milking machines; yet the Amish community in Arthur, Illinois (which uses horsepower to farm) does allow them. Some communities draw their water with windmill power, others draw it by hand from a well or pump, and others use modern plumbing. Refrigerators are used in most Iowa communities, although they are powered by kerosene or gas, not electricity.

problems in Amish culture

It is dangerous to romanticize the Amish. Any community will have its problems, and the Amish are no exception. The Amish today face many pressures: the economic pressure of living a technology-free life in an increasingly technological-driven world, the pressure of making a living as a small farmer in an age of the big farm, the pressure of conforming to their own strict rules of conduct.

Conforming to Amish codes of conduct can create both security and tension. Although the Amish are famous for their willingness to help each other in times of need, they can be punitive in enforcing conformity on their church members.

Those who respect the Ordnung enjoy security, brotherly love, contentment, equality, unity, togetherness and fellowship, and the strengthening of marital and family ties.

However, if baptized members deviate from the Ordnung in some way, they may be excommunicated for lack of faith. Once excommunicated, the person falls under "the ban," or *Meidung*, which means that he or she is shunned by all others in the church. If church members seem to be making too much money, are taking too much pride in possessions, or in any way are not following the Ordnung, they may be shunned.

This practice of shunning seems severe to outsiders, because the shunned person is not allowed to eat or talk with the rest of the family until he or she asks for forgiveness before the whole congregation. Once accepted back into the faith, though, it is said that the person is not stigmatized and the misdeed is never mentioned to him or her.

A different problem faces young people who do not feel that they fit into Amish society. With only an eighth-grade education, they are not prepared to do anything other than carpentry, farming, housekeeping, or manual labor. Disenchanted young people must leave behind everything and everyone they know and find their way in a foreign world.

A common solution to internal or social pressure is to join another Anabaptist group with a more liberal lifestyle, such as the

Mennonites. In many communities, Amish family members who join another church are not shunned, although they can never be a close member of the family or Amish community again.

Another remedy is to move to a more tolerant Amish community. Sociologists call this option the "safety valve" in Amish society, allowing differences of opinion to be expressed in a socially acceptable way.

Whenever a group of individuals become dissatisfied with the Ordnung of their district (for being either too liberal or too conservative), they can join another district that suits their views or can start fresh in a new location with like-minded friends. Historically, an abundance of open land in America provided the Amish with freedom to move whenever a community's internal tensions became too great.

Other problems of Amish culture include the limited gene pool. The three main Amish settlements in the United States (in Pennsylvania, Ohio, and Indiana) virtually have a closed gene pool, because they usually marry Amish partners from within their own communities. More than half of the population of these communities share five family names, and certain genetic diseases are more prevalent.

These genetic diseases do not appear to be as much of a problem in smaller Amish communities, where young people cannot always find suitable spouses close by and are more likely to marry Amish church members from outside their immediate community.

In many other ways the Amish are healthier than other Americans. Although mental illness and suicide do occur in Amish communities, the rate of suicide among the Amish in Lancaster County is half the rate for rural people in the United States.[1] Hypertension among the Lancaster County Amish is rare, and their average blood pressure is lower than other agrarian populations. Cervical cancer in Amish women is less frequent than in women in other rural populations in the United States.

In today's fragmented world, the Amish are probably more respected and admired than at any other time in history. Overwhelmed with hyperconsumerism and runaway technology, many people think nostalgically about returning to the morals and rural lifestyle enjoyed by most Americans just 100 years ago.

Beleaguered parents and burned-out professionals are drawn to the Amish because of their close family and community relationships, their commitment to shelter both children and the elderly, their nonviolent, religion-based way of life, their tradition of providing neighborly aid in a crisis, and their use of restraints to control the detrimental influences of technology. Each of these qualities is fast disappearing in modern life. Surely much can be learned from the Amish.

note

1. Donald B. Kraybill, John A. Hostetler and D.G. Shaw, "Suicide Patterns in a Religious Subculture: The Old Order Amish," *International Journal of Moral and Social Studies* I (Autumn 1968).

part one

 home

chapter

1

at home with the Herschbergers

*A*t *the center of Amish life is the family, and families are large and tight-knit. The typical home reflects the Amish belief in the simple life: it's usually painted plain white with no trim, has simple furnishings and plain wood or linoleum floors, and is tidy. Quilting frames and young children playing with toys often fill living rooms. A typical Amish home is large enough to accommodate a family of 10 or 12.*

Although the Amish believe in old-fashioned discipline, I observed that an abundance of love filled the home. Younger children were readily scooped into the lap of an older sister or parent, and each child was treated with respect, kindness, and dignity. Fathers seemed equally affectionate with babies and toddlers as mothers were.

Children learn early to help their younger siblings. I once saw a five-year-old boy patiently help his three-year-old sister find her lost doll—and then carefully close the stairway door to prevent her from accidentally falling down the stairs. He had obviously been taught how to take care of her. New babies are welcomed as a gift from God, and infants become the center of love and affection in an Amish home.

Children also learn to respect the elderly, who seldom end their lives in lonely nursing homes. Grandparents usually turn the farm over to their youngest son after he marries and has children, and move into a smaller house on the property, called a grossdadi, *or "grandfather," house. The grandparents continue to work on the farm as they grow older, surrounded by their many grandchildren and enjoying the love and respect of the whole family.*

A child growing up in an Amish family could seldom feel lonely, being surrounded by brothers and sisters—and lots of relatives. I once visited an Amish home and saw a cloth birthday calendar on the wall with 10 or 12 names written under each month. "Those are our cousins' birthdays," said the Amish girl who lived there. "But only on my mother's side. There's another calendar upstairs for the cousins on my father's side." This girl had more than 250 cousins! As one Amish man told me, "Just being someone's cousin doesn't mean you get invited to their wedding—there just isn't enough room."

It could be any farm in Drakesville, Iowa: a large white house, four neatly painted green farm buildings, and a half-acre garden asleep for the winter. Two black buggies sitting idle in the open shed reveal that an Amish family lives here.

Monroe Herschberger smiles and offers a strong handshake. He wears the traditional Amish clothing—a work shirt, suspenders, and plain denim pants. Eddie, a shy boy of 13, and Andy Ray, nine, look like miniature versions of their father, minus the beard. Monroe and his sons have the same haircut—as if someone put a bowl on their heads and trimmed around it.

Like many Amish households, the entry to the house is through the kitchen. Monroe's wife, Mary, smiles warmly and introduces their daughters, Mandy, age 11, Erma, age 16, and Wilma, age 18. Like their mother, the girls wear plain, high-neck dresses fastened with straight pins, and they tuck their hair neatly under white prayer caps.

They invite me for a tour of the house. A quilting frame, stretched with green polyester fabric, fills one side of the living room. Mary and her older daughters have made the tiny, painstaking stitches that crisscross the quilt.

A finely crafted oak cabinet stands beside a large window. "That was my mother's," says Mary shyly.

It's warm inside the house, despite the cold weather. Monroe has built his own wood stove in the corner, using an empty oil drum propped on four legs above a bed of white stone.

"Most winter days, it's almost too hot," says Mary.

To see at night, the family uses gas or kerosene lanterns. To show me, Mary lights a lantern with a long kitchen match. The filament radiates a bright, powerful light. She points to the hook in the ceiling where they hang the lamp to provide light for the whole room.

An example of Monroe's ingenuity sits under the window. It is a modern sewing machine, complete with buttonholer and zigzag stitching. Monroe tilts it to show that it has no motor—he converted it to a treadle machine. Mary and her older daughters, Erma and Wilma, sew most of the family's clothing on the machine.

Monroe adapted the refrigerator in the kitchen to run on kerosene fuel. When I ask why kerosene is allowed but electricity is not, Monroe answers, "Have you ever known any group of people to live without rules? We base our rules and regulations on the Bible. I know what I could expect to get from the world, and I know there is a lot more contentment here at home. I equal it out in my mind, and even though we give up some things, I'm more satisfied with what we've got."

Adjoining the living room is the master bedroom. A beautiful cedar chest sits at the foot of the bed, another heirloom from Mary's mother. Monroe lifts the white crocheted bedspread to show me the waterbed and wooden frame he constructed. He gave them to Mary on her birthday a few years ago.

"Monroe was wanting a waterbed for quite a while," Mary teases.

On Sundays when they have church in their home, the Herschbergers move their furniture aside and seat the congregation in the bedroom and living room on wooden benches. Monroe purposely built the doorway between the rooms extra-wide, so the bishop can stand in the middle and speak to crowds in both places. Eventually Monroe plans to replace the wall with a sliding door to make it even easier to host church or large gatherings such as weddings.

Upstairs there are two more bedrooms, one for the two boys and a larger one for the three girls. The rooms are tidy and simple, with bare floors, dressers, and closets.

The family frequently visits with their relatives on holidays. For one family reunion, two busloads of Mary's family traveled from Illinois to Iowa to visit. "I like having a big house, because at Christmas we can sleep 30 relatives," says Mary.

Mary invites me into the living room to chat. I select a straight-backed chair, and the five children crowd together on a couch with their parents. Mary passes around a huge metal bowl of popcorn, homegrown in their garden last year.

Monroe amuses us with his jokes and stories. "I once went to a chiropractor who asked me how many brothers and sisters I have. I told him that I have five brothers and each of them have eight sisters! You should have seen the look on his face." Monroe actually has 13 brothers and sisters.

While Monroe and Mary talk with me in their easy and comfortable way, the children speak only when I directly address them. Mandy reads a book.

"They love to read," says Mary. "That's why we have so many books." She nods toward the bookshelf.

When Mary speaks to Mandy in German, Mandy sighs and

sets down her book reluctantly. Yet she obediently fetches Mary's glasses, just as she was asked.

When I mention how well behaved the children are, Monroe teases, "Weeelll, they're good around company!"

The Herschberger's two oldest sons have already left home. Of the remaining children, only Mandy, Andy Ray, and Eddie are still in school. Having finished all eight grades of an Amish education, Erma and Wilma work at home helping their mother.

"Amish children start working with their parents at a young age," says Monroe. "They're used to hard work. It's part of their life."

Because Monroe must work off the farm at a carpentry job to meet their mortgage payments, the girls help with the farming. With their mother, they plow the family's half-acre garden and the cornfields with a team of workhorses, and they manually collect thousands of eggs from their henhouse two times each day.

Monroe tells me he'd much rather work at home on the farm, "which is in my childhood blood." He leaves the house at 6:30 a.m. and returns at 6:30 p.m. On Saturdays, he does farm chores and catches up with farmwork, and on Sundays, the whole family rests.

"I often think it's a good thing I was born Amish," says Monroe, "because I'd be too lazy to work on Sunday."

Monroe offers to take me on a buggy ride and sends Andy Ray out to hitch up one of the family's 15 horses to their black buggy.

Outside, I am properly introduced to June, the shaggy, black horse who pulls the buggy. Monroe sits in front and drives, while I sit in back with Andy Ray.

Monroe heads the buggy toward the schoolhouse a mile down the road. As June trots onto the highway, Monroe lets one wooden wheel roll onto the shoulder.

"This is how we keep from going too fast down hills," he explains. At first the cool winter air is pleasant as it rushes through the open windows, but as we pick up speed and the wind whips us in the face, Monroe closes the canopy windows in front. I feel protected and safe inside, and I like the way I can see out but others can't see in.

If it were much colder or raining, Monroe could snap down the black oilcloth flaps that keep rain and cold from seeping in, making the buggy snug and dark. Lap blankets help keep passengers warm in winter, and some Amish families cover the floor of their buggies with horse blankets to keep their feet toasty when the weather is cold.

"They don't make horse equipment anymore, so we just patch up, fix up, and make do with what we've got," comments Monroe as he slaps the reins. "If you can figure out how to fix these, you can figure out how to fix anything."

Monroe parks the buggy outside the small shed that shelters the children's ponies and horses on school days. We enter the one-room schoolhouse the children attend through eighth grade.

"A lot of non-Amish farmers would like to send their own children here," says Monroe. "They see that our children are disciplined and orderly. When children have the same teacher as they grow up, the teacher knows them better."

The 14 old-fashioned wooden desks, complete with inkwells and attached seats, look well used. They are arranged in neat rows. A reciting bench is placed next to the teacher's desk, so one class can recite their lessons while the others work on assignments. Written on the blackboard is a psalm from the Bible. A helper's chart with words like "obedience" and "service," along with the children's names, hangs on one wall. The scholars' careful handwriting covers another. A sign advises, "If you have something to say about someone else, you should say it as if he were listening."

We head home. After a tour of the barn, Mary invites me back into the house, where the children have taken turns churning the handle on the ice cream maker. I chat with Monroe and Mary in the kitchen, savoring the rich flavor of homemade vanilla ice cream long after the others have finished.

The five children, who have drifted into the dining hall, start singing "Silent Night" in German.

When I watch them sing another song they learned at school, it's clear they are not shy about singing and have had lots of practice. They smile and sing the words clearly and boldly.

Three miles west of Drakesville, Iowa,
A little down the gravel road
Dwell a gang of willing workers
In a pretty white abode.
Oh we little children dwelling
In our one-room country school,
Ought to please our teacher gaily;
Listen and obey each rule.

Paul, Jacob, Perry, Freeman,
Harley, Kenneth, John Henry,
Eddie, Ivan, Erwin, Leroy,
Vernon, Jonas, Andy Ray.
The girls are Mandy, Erma,
Linda, Naomi, Mary, Edna Mae,
LeAnne, Lucy, Leona,
Loretta and Lena Mae.

Teacher says it's sure a pleasure
Hearing little children sing;
So come on let's sing together
Make our voices really ring.
Monday, Tuesday, Wednesday, Thursday,
Friday in the schoolhouse dwell
Seeking for our education
Hoping all things work out well.

After the singing is over, I say good-bye. The Herschbergers have shared their easy laughter and warm hearts. They stand at the door as I leave the farm laden with gifts: bags of homegrown popcorn, jars of dill pickles made from cucumbers grown on the farm, and a taste of the simple charm of Amish life.

The Budget, a weekly paper established in 1890, circulates to all the Amish and Mennonite communities in North America (and a few in South America, too). A reporter from each community submits a weekly report, including births, deaths, visits, and anecdotes, keeping everyone informed of happenings in other communities. Everyone reads *The Budget,* because without telephones, it's the easiest way to keep up with friends and family who live far away. Here are a few excerpts.

CHOTEAO, OK
Mayes Co.
Nov. 24—Temp. in lower 30s and is sleeting. There's no way to describe how it looks. The trees, fences—guess you'd say everything out there—has a coat of ice. The flowers that weren't frozen are hanging their heads.

Menfolks are helping put up dairy barns, adding onto houses, and the most important of all (that is for some) is the deer season is open. I'm sure that more have gotten one, but the only one I heard of is Floyd Schrock, got a doe.

They are planning to have a surprise 10th wedding anniversary shower at Glen Yoders' tomorrow for Levi and Edna Faye Yoder.

Being the weather was like it was, Bill and Cassie Detweiler and Mose and Sue Yoder just stayed home [from church] today.

LUDINGTON, MI
Nov. 25—27° this morning with a light blanket of snow on the ground again, and sunshine. Received the snow yesterday.

The non-Amish neighbor bought a heifer recently at a sale, which seemed to have been someone's pet. But it did not want to yield to authority and butted him down, in over the electric fence. Thankfully he wasn't seriously hurt.

Nov. 25—Nice sunny day. Still have a snow cover.

There are still quite a few items left at Melvin Beachys' when the funeral was there. Among the items are a stainless steel mixing bowl and big spoon, stainless steel cake pan lid, a black montley with a cape, black voile cap, flashlight and white plastic pan with lid.

Ervin Yutzys' found a 2-buckle overshoe on the road. The owner can pick it up at Ervin's.

Miss Alma Gingerich has the Nature's Sunshine products in her home now, taking over from Mrs. Chris Miller.

Eli and Diane Yoder have another girl, named Anna. She joins 2 brothers and 2 sisters.

Henry J. Yoder, who was in the hospital over a week, is now out of intensive care.

chapter

2

milking a two-bucket cow

*T*he Amish love to farm. *"I think I wouldn't want to be living if I weren't on a farm,"* an Amish teenager once told me. *"It's exciting—there's always something happening."*

Farming is also a way to keep the family together. When the father works at home, he can take an active role in raising the children, training them in the Amish way of life.

The Amish believe that farmers live closest to God. "On a farm, you can see that God is in all things that are alive and growing," explains Leah Peachy, an Amish woman I met in North Carolina.

They are also known to be excellent farmers. Centuries ago, while still in Europe, the Amish were often banned from land ownership and were forced to farm land so poor that no one else wanted it. In order to survive, they experimented with new methods, such as crop rotation. The Old Order Amish today still practice a four-year crop rotation system in Iowa and other states, planting corn for two years, oats for one year, and a hay crop the fourth year.

The Amish feel that they are not the owners of their land. Rather, they are caretakers entrusted with the use of the soil. They carefully nourish their fields—preferring organic fertilizers such as manure—so that when they retire the land is as healthy as when they began. If an Amish man damages the soil, he is considered to be as sinful as a thief. As a result, Amish farms are extremely fertile and productive.

This chapter introduces the Yoder family, who appear in other chapters in the book. The first time I met Nancy Yoder she came to the door of her large white farmhouse to greet me. She had been quilting with her daughter Annie, then 17. There was a calmness and orderliness about her and her home. It was hard to believe that she was the mother of nine children, with one more on the way, living on a farm without electricity, telephone, automobile, or automatic washing machine. With three children married or working and three children in school, she spent her days working at home with Annie and her sister Regina. They helped her care for Leah, a preschooler. And a few months later, when baby Wayne was born, they helped her care for him.

I found the same serene and well-managed homes at other Amish farms. With Amish schools within walking distance, schoolchildren can walk to school or drive themselves in the pony cart, freeing mothers from the suburban tribulation of driving children around town. I never saw an Amish person rushing, although Amish families work hard all year-round and are especially busy during harvest and planting times. Both adults and children go about their tasks in a focused way but without a feeling of pressure. With so many to help, it seems no one is ever left alone with too hard of a job.

Golden sunlight stretches wide over the Iowa hayfields in early September. At the Yoder farm near Bloomfield, a girl waves a hearty hello.

This is Regina, age 15. Besides household chores, she and her older sister Annie milk their family's cows and drive a team of horses in the fields.

The girls laugh merrily when they talk. "Some people think we are twins, especially when we dress the same," says Annie with a laugh. Today they wear identical raspberry-colored dresses, white aprons, and royal blue scarves tied under their chins.

Both say they'd rather spend their day in the fields than inside the house. "I think it's great fun to work out," says Regina.

"I feel more free outside," agrees Annie in her mild way. "Farm-work doesn't have to be done so fine and neat as needlework."

Their day starts at 6:00 a.m, when their father wakes up the eight children who still live at home. Before breakfast, the girls feed the cows while their father and 22-year-old brother, Dan, feed the horses. All four help with the milking, and then Dan goes off to work as a carpenter.

The 12 black-and-white spotted Holsteins all look identical to me, but the girls befriended Jody, Joline, Vera, Abby, Shirley, Tina, Sheila, Fannie, and Pam when they were calves and call each one by name. Honey Lou and Sunny Sue, two fawn-colored Jerseys munching hay in the corner, complete their herd.

Do the cows ever kick?

"Some people's cows do kick, but ours don't," says Regina. "If they start to kick, we give them a little slap and they learn they can't do that." Hobbles—clamps that gently draw the cow's hind legs together just above the knee—keep the cows quiet during milking.

Sometimes the girls do get stepped on, which is not too serious. "It hurts for about five minutes, and that's all there is to it," says Regina.

Inside the barn I meet two colts, Dawn and Beauty. Regina pats Beauty on the lips, who bares her teeth in a jack-o-lantern smile. "I like to tease her," says Regina mischievously. "She bit me the other day, just to be playful. Boy, did that hurt."

An immense black stallion stands in the stalls across from the colts. "He's gentle," Regina reassures me as she strokes his forehead between soft black eyes. "He helps us clean the barn in the winter by pulling the manure spreader while we pile it up."

Suddenly three wide-eyed children appear. Robert, David, and Grace, aged seven, 10, and 12, just drove home from their one-room school in an open pony cart. They show me how to hitch it up. Like a well-trained team, Robert and David pull the cart out of the shed while Grace slips the bridle on Midnight, their pony, and backs him in between the cart's shafts. In one minute, thanks to teamwork, it's ready to go. Annie takes me for a ride. The wind blows in our faces. Annie likes riding in a cart better than a buggy, she says, "because it's more open, more free." We pass the grassy pasture where the Yoder's cows and horses graze peacefully. With just a slight tug, Midnight turns around.

Back on the farm, I notice the family's three black, covered buggies stored in an open shed. Annie and Regina have driven their family's covered buggies to town or to visit friends "since we were big enough to reach up and put the bridle on the horse," says Annie.

The family owns two Standard Bred geldings to pull the buggies and nine big-boned Percheron mares to plow the fields. Both girls love to mow the hay fields with a team of two mares. "If you like horses, you like to do things with them," says Annie.

"Driving a workhorse is even more fun than driving a gelding, because they're more powerful," says Regina. "When you drive the team, you just feel content. Except you have to watch to make sure you're at the row you should be and the mower doesn't get jammed up."

The geldings and massive draft horses are easy to handle and calm, the girls tell me. "We do have one pony that is kind of skittish," says Regina. "So only Dad or Dan [her older brother] rides him."

Soon it's 5:00 p.m. and time for Regina to round up the horses and cows from the pasture. Barefoot, she rides Midnight without a saddle, because "Dad says it's more fun to ride bareback."

The sun slips low on the horizon by the time the cows are in their stalls. In a graceful motion, Annie swings the hobble chain under a cow named Sheila and fastens it just above the knees, drawing them together.

"Usually, you milk cows on the right side," Annie says. But since Sheila is a two-bucket cow, the girls place their stools on opposite sides of Sheila, clutch shiny metal pails between their legs, and pull the cow's teats with both hands in brisk rhythm. Frothy milk splashes into the buckets.

"Want to try?" Annie asks. I do, but when I squeeze the cow's udder, there's barely a trickle. Annie laughs and makes milk squirt like a faucet.

They like to sing while milking. A plaintive hymn floats in the air, voices clear and sweet, perfectly on key.

> There are no shadows
> Without the sunshine.
> There are no showers
> When all is fair.
> And roses blooming
> In thorny places
> With sweetest fragrance
> Perfume the air.

Grace joins in, Robert listens. David stretches full-length on top of Midnight, stroking his mane and gazing dreamily out the window. It's a moment of contentment, a moment I want to go on forever, suspended in time. But with milking over, Queenie the collie herds the spotted cows out of the barnyard. Regina shuts the gate, and the family is ready for dinner and bed.

After my visit, Annie and Regina wrote these letters to me.

Dear Linda,
Greetings of Love!
Thank you so much for the candy! We received it in today's mail. We are very pleased with your story. Everything is

worded so nice.

We have a couple of words we want to change, but not much. On page 2 where the hobbles draw the cow's hind legs together—just below the knee. It's above, not below. Page 3 put the bridle on the horses, not halter.

That's all we found that's wrong.

Today we did the laundry and picked a 5-gallon bucket full of green beans, so we have to can those tomorrow. THANKS again for the candy!

Bye

Annie

And on the other side of the paper:

Dear Linda:

Greetings of Love!

First of all, I want to thank you for the candy. It was very good. And we were very pleased with the way you wrote the story. It was worded just *perfectly*. There were a few words wrong but nothing much, and I see Annie has corrected them. But she forgot something on the 2nd page in the 3rd paragraph. About the cows, you must have forgotten the 2 Jersey's names, Honey Lou and Sunny Sue.

Thanks again for the candy.

Bye

Regina

✳

by foot, by horse, by buggy

The black horse-drawn buggy is a familiar sight in Amish communities. Families usually travel by covered buggy on the way to church, the country store, a quilting, or anywhere in the community up to 10 miles away.

In Iowa, Amish buggies are square at the top but tapered at the bottom. Black paint coats the wooden sides, and a large orange triangle on the back of each buggy warns automobile drivers of a slow-moving vehicle. The shapes and colors of buggies may vary in different communities. For instance, while all Iowa buggies are black, buggies in Pennsylvania may also be white, yellow, or brown. Most communities have their own buggy makers, and it takes as much as 100 hours to make one.

Although the Amish shun anything fancy, they don't mind buying healthy, spirited horses to pull their vehicles. The Amish are known for their finely bred "drivers" (the horses that pull carts and buggies), which they buy at auctions. Most Amish choose Standard Bred horses, raised for racing, as drivers.

When a teenage boy receives his first buggy at age 16, he enters the stage of "rum springa," which means literally "jumping around" or "running around." During this time before taking the vows to join the church, the Amish youth has a bit more freedom. It is said that parents look the other way if a young man buys a radio for his buggy, decorates it with "fancy" bumper stickers or decals, or occasionally races it down a country road, hoping to beat his best friend. In some larger communities, teenage boys may even secretly buy a car, which is forbidden by the Amish as being too worldly. Once the youth gets baptized and enters the church, he must settle down and follow the plain way of life of his parents.

Most large Amish families own several buggies. Other forms of transportation include the open spring buggy, which has cushioned seats but no covering, and thus it can only be driven in good weather. The pony cart is a favorite vehicle for schoolchildren to drive to school. It's low to the ground and has only two wheels and a single board for a seat. Horse-drawn sleighs are a cozy way to traverse the roads in winter. One family I met had built a "double buggy," which featured an extra seat of soft velveteen so the whole family could travel to church together.

I once asked a young Amish boy of 13 how he got around, and he smiled and said, "My feet!" He said the farthest he had ever walked was three-and-a-half miles, to his grandfather's farm. When I asked him how long it took, he said simply, "We weren't in a hurry, so we didn't time ourselves." He and his brothers and sisters walked the half-mile to and from school each day.

Although the Amish do not fly in airplanes, you may see an Amish family ride by bus, train, or hired van. That's how they travel long distances to visit relatives or to attend weddings and funerals in other states. They also might occasionally hire a van to go see a doctor or to attend an auction in a nearby town if the distance is too far to travel in a buggy.

It's not that they're against riding in cars, one Amish man explained, it's just that if everyone owned a car, it would destroy their community. If you drive a horse and buggy, you stay closer to home and family and you rely more on your neighbors and local merchants for your needs. The horse and buggy has become a symbol of the Amish belief that they should be "in the world but not of it."

Excerpt from *The Budget:*

OAKFIELD, ME
Beyond Mattawamkeag
Sun., Aug. 4—The Chris Hilty family drove over to the

Woodstock, New Brunswick community for church services with their horse and buggy, a distance of around 22 miles one way. They started at 5:20 Sun. morning and, since New Brunswick is one time zone ahead of Maine, they arrived a few minutes late for services. They returned home Sun. evening.

Over last weekend Isaac Kup, one of the boys from Tenn., drove over to New Brunswick with one of the horses and our road cart. The other 2 boys, Wade Jewitt and Jacob Hochstetler, rode their bicycles. They left Sat. after dinner and came back Mon.

I'm sure the customs people at the border find it a bit unusual to have horse-drawn vehicles come through customs. No doubt they even find it somewhat intriguing. So far they have not caused us any problems crossing the border with our horses.

chapter

3

cooking in the Yoder's summer kitchen

*T*he Amish are famous for their cooking. While some recipes come from German and Swiss ancestors, many meals resemble traditional American farm fare—meat, potatoes, homemade bread, garden vegetables, biscuits and gravy, and a baked dessert. The food varies slightly from region to region. For instance, shoofly pie, made from molasses and eggs, is a famous Amish dessert in Pennsylvania. But Annie and Regina Yoder's family from Bloomfield, Iowa, had never heard of it.

Although they shun material comforts, the Amish do not skimp on food. Because most families work up an appetite laboring on the farm, they enjoy three large and tasty meals a day, starting with a robust hot breakfast. Homemade baked goods are an important part of the Amish diet. Fresh homemade bread appears at most meals, and cakes, pies, or cookies are never lacking.

Food plays an important role at any Amish gathering, and each guest brings something to contribute to the meal. Since they believe in being as self-sufficient as possible, the Amish raise most food on their own farms—fresh eggs from chickens, milk from cows, vegetables from gardens, fruits from orchards, grains from fields, and meat from farm animals. Even popcorn grows in the garden. It's common to see bundles of popcorn, tied in white muslin, hanging from front porch eaves to dry.

Amish gardens are vast—covering as much as one acre. While the women are usually in charge of the garden, often the whole family pitches in for weeding and planting. In the gardens I saw, the plants lined up in neat rows. Amish women usually plant plenty of bright-colored flowers to line the edges. In a typical Amish garden, not a weed shows its head.

Because they raise all of their vegetables in their garden—eating them fresh in the summer and canning them for winter meals—their food is mostly organic.

To find out more about Amish cooking, I visited my friends Annie, Regina, and Grace Yoder. For some dishes, the Yoder girls follow recipes. For others, such as hash brown potatoes or salad dressing, they do it "by guess."

It's late morning when I arrive at the Yoder house one hot June day. The whole family spent the morning picking strawberries from their large garden. I can tell by the red ring around his mouth that even baby Wayne helped out.

A huge metal bowl—holding 15 quarts of strawberries—sits on the counter inside the Yoder's kitchen. The girls tell me they usually add sugar to make strawberry topping, but ran out this morning. So their mother and father just left for town in their horse and buggy to pick up some sugar.

"Strawberries take a lot of sugar!" says Regina. "Mom's going to take these berries over to our neighbor lady, just to be neighborly, I guess." Last week, the family picked 26 quarts and froze them.

Since it's 11:00 in the morning, the girls begin to prepare dinner, their main meal of the day.

Grace washes and tears apart some fresh leaf lettuce. "It's from our sister Mary Edna's garden," says Annie. "This year we couldn't plant lettuce because it rained so much. But my sister's garden is on a slope, so she could get hers in."

Annie mixes a meatloaf using beef they butchered last fall. Regina peels potatoes and shows me how to poke the potatoes into a crank-style stainless steel shredder without getting my fingers nicked.

While we cook, four-year-old Leah plays with Wayne. "I'm gonna get you!" she gently teases as she trots behind him at his toddler's speed. He squeals with delight.

In the large Yoder kitchen, long and wide counters provide spacious work areas for all the daughters. There's also plenty of room for a large wooden table, where the family gathers for meals. A wooden hutch holds two sets of delicately flowered china, saved for weddings.

A cloth covers the giant wood-burning stove and oven. "We use this wood stove only in the winter, because it gives off so much heat," says Annie. In summer, they cook on a kerosene range that sits in the large entry porch, so the kitchen stays cool.

After Grace lights the kerosene stove, Regina scrapes her shredded potatoes into a cast-iron skillet with some shortening and sets the burner on low. She explains that you have to cook hash browns slowly or the potatoes don't get done. "We think putting a lid on helps keep them softer, too," she says. Annie places her meatloaf in a small square metal oven that sits on top of one burner.

Regina pries a lid off a jar of string beans, making a popping noise. The Yoders can their own homegrown, organic vegetables. She places the beans in a pan and heats them.

Regina shows me where the canned vegetables are stored, down the wooden steps in a cool basement. She sets Wayne down at the foot of the stairs. He smiles when his bare feet touch cool cement.

We peek into the root cellar, a separate room dug out of the earth and lined with bricks. On one side, the shelves contain jars of peas, beans, corn, tomatoes, pizza sauce, applesauce, peaches, pears, and cherries.

On the other side, gleaming glass jars crowd the shelves. At this time of the year, the number of empty jars far outnumbers the full ones. It's only a few weeks until harvest and all the jars will be filled again.

Upstairs again, Annie discovers she can't make the salad dressing without the sugar. The girls aren't sure if their parents will get back by the time the meal starts.

"I'll ride the pony to Mary Edna's," says Regina. Their married sister lives down the road, and she will loan them a cup of sugar.

"As soon as she leaves, Mom and Dad will return from town," predicts Annie in her understated way. Which pretty much happens. They all arrive at once, Regina barefoot on her pony and Mom and Dad in their horse and buggy.

The children's mother, Nancy, greets me and pulls off her heavy black bonnet, which she wears over her white prayer cap when she goes to town or to church. Her face is flushed from the heat.

Toby, the children's father, saunters in from the barn with a big smile. Like many Amish men, he looks younger than his age, with cheeks a healthy rose color and dark hair showing no signs of gray. We chat for a few moments. He says that they purchased the farm from an "English" farmer nine years ago.

"At first, nothing would grow unless we poured lots of chemicals on it," says Toby. By rotating the crops and by using manure for fertilizer, he revived the soil and can now farm almost without chemicals.

By 12:30, all nine of us bow our heads in silent thanks to God. Wayne sits quietly in his mother's lap. I look up to see fresh, healthy faces lining both sides of the table.

A bounty of string beans, meatloaf, hash browns, homemade bread, and salad pass my way. Everything tastes delicious. The salad dressing, Nancy tells me, is made from an old family recipe. It's a perfect combination of sweet and sour—mustard, mayonnaise, and sugar. For a spectacular dessert, we pour fresh strawberry sauce over bowls of homemade chocolate cake and Little Debbie oatmeal cookies, topping all that with fresh cream, collected just hours before.

"We like to sing while we do the dishes," says Annie after dinner. She selects one of her favorite songs, "As a Life of a Flower," from a hand-copied songbook. She perches the book over the sink in a holder made from a bent coat hanger, so it's easy to see the words while she washes the dishes. Regina, Grace, and I sing along while we dry the dishes. In some places, the three sisters sing different parts, their voices weaving in and out like swallows swooping by the barnyard.

As the life of a flower,
be our lives pure and sweet.
May we brighten the way,
for the friends that we greet.
And sweet incense arise,
from our hearts as we give.
Close to Him He doth teach us
to love and forgive.

I return home with a quart of fresh strawberries and the last Little Debbie, nourished by bountiful food and light spirits.

Debbie's oatmeal cookies (Little Debbies)

3 c. brown sugar (scant)	4 eggs
1 1/2 c. margarine	1 1/2 tsp. soda
1/2 tsp. salt	1 tsp. cinnamon
4 c. oatmeal	1 1/2 c. flour

Mix in order given. Drop by tsp. on a greased cookie sheet. Flatten with spoon dipped in water. Bake at 375°. These cookies bake fast. Do not overbake.

Filling: 1 c. powdered sugar, 1 beaten egg white, 1/2 c. Crisco,
1 Tbsp. vanilla.

Place filling between two cookies.

—Mrs. John Miller

From: *Amish Country Cooking,* 1989. To order a copy, write
Andy and Millie Yoder, 466 W. Kootenal, Rexford, MT
59930.

✳

Once while visiting an Amish home I noticed a
number of strange notations on the calendar. It turns
out that the teenage daughter had marked out the
steps for making friendship bread. It's customary for
friends to pass on the starter for this sourdough
bread, making it a special way to express love and
companionship.

friendship bread

Days 1 and 2	Do nothing. (Let the starter sit in its covered container on the counter.)
Day 3	Stir with wooden spoon.
Days 4 and 5	Do nothing.
Day 6	Add 1 c. milk, 1 c. flour, 1 c. sugar and stir.
Day 7	Do nothing.
Day 8	Stir with wooden spoon.
Day 9	Do nothing.
Day 10	Add 1 c. milk, 1. c. flour, 1 c. sugar and stir.

Then put 1 cup of batter into each of three containers; keep
one and give two away with this recipe.

In the remaining batter add: 2/3 c. oil or butter, 1/2 c. milk,
3 eggs, 1 Tbsp. vanilla.

In separate bowl mix:

2 c. flour

1 1/2 c. sugar

1 1/2 tsp. baking powder

3 Tbsp. cornstarch

2 tsp. vanilla

2 tsp. cinnamon

3/4 tsp. soda

1 c. nuts

Butter two loaf pans. Pour batter into both pans and sprinkle with cinnamon and sugar. Bake at 400° for 40 to 50 minutes, until golden brown. Enjoy!

part two

❧ school ❧
and
work

chapter

4

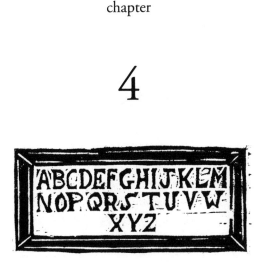

learning the three Rs

*A*mish children complete their formal schooling at the eighth grade. Amish schools look much like the rural one-room schoolhouses most Americans attended a century ago. In small white wooden buildings on country roads, all eight grades learn their lessons in one room. Amish students, called scholars, learn the "three Rs"—reading, writing and arithmetic.

Even though the teachers are Amish and have earned only an eighth-grade education themselves, Amish schools have been highly successful in teaching children the necessary skills to run an efficient farm and conduct a profitable business. A farmer must know geometry, for instance, to design a new barn. An Amish businessman must be able to multiply and divide without a calculator.

Virtually no illiteracy exists among the Amish. In one study, Amish children scored equal to or higher than other rural children *on the* Iowa Test of Basic Skills *in spelling, reading, and arithmetic.*[1]

This is remarkable considering that English is a second language to these children, who speak a German dialect as their mother tongue and learn English only when they enter first grade. All school lessons are conducted in English, because the Amish want their children to be able to converse comfortably with English-speaking neighbors and businessmen.

Amish schools teach the values that the Amish cherish: discipline, respect, and cooperation. The classes I visited were far more orderly and focused than any modern ones I've seen. I also noticed that these children were accustomed to behaving in a disciplined manner, without requiring much attention from the teacher. No cloud of fear hung over the classroom, and they moved about freely, without asking for permission when they needed to go to the outhouse or leave their seats. Amish children know what the rules are and never have the opportunity to say, "But Johnny's parents let him do it!" because Amish parents, teachers, and neighbors consistently reinforce the same ideals.

Amish scholars learn to help younger children with their schoolwork. The Amish value helping each other more than competing and doing the job right more than speed. Amish children spend the greater part of each day drilling, memorizing, and reciting.

Parents and teachers encourage the scholars not to rush over their work. Do not be like the world, they teach, but be contented. Hurry will only lead to lack of satisfaction.

T he air snaps with the sharpness of autumn as I ride down a country road near Bloomfield, Iowa, in an open pony cart. I'm cozily packed in with the Yoder children—Grace, Robert, and David, who holds the reins. A truck rumbles by, kicking up dust and gravel.

Midnight slows to a walk as we climb the last hill to the schoolhouse. I'm worried that she is straining, unaccustomed to my extra weight.

But David says, "I'm glad she has a load this morning. It keeps her from acting silly and shying." Grace explains that "shying" means veering into the ditch beside the road.

"We must be late," says David. "They're already putting up the net." Just outside the white one-room wooden Amish schoolhouse, we see two children tying a volleyball net between the swing set and a buggy. Pleasant Hill School doesn't actually start until 9:00 a.m., but the children like to get there early to play volleyball and other games.

When we arrive, David and Grace swiftly unhitch the pony, and David leads Midnight into the barn, where the horses patiently stand while the children are in school. A horse cart, an open buggy, and two black, covered buggies already crowd the schoolyard.

Grace takes me inside to meet the two schoolteachers, who teach all eight grades in one room. Ruth Graber, a young woman of 20 with rosy cheeks and steady, clear blue eyes, greets me. She wears a modest brown dress, her fine blond hair neatly contained under a white prayer cap. Ruth teaches the second, sixth, seventh, and eighth graders. Her co-teacher, 19-year-old Rachel Mast, has dark hair and soft brown eyes that shine through her glasses. She instructs the first, third, and fourth graders. No children attend fifth grade this year.

Ruth invites me to look around, and says that I can walk about freely even after classes start.

A wooden floor and rows of windows looking out onto the fields give the room a pleasant, homey feeling. A brightly colored display reads, "Stepping Stones to a Good School Year: Do your best, have neat papers, be polite, have good posture, be on time, don't whisper." Twenty-five signs, carefully crayoned by the 25 children in the school, tell the reader to "Do unto others as you would have them do onto you." Neat rows of colorful name cards, spelling charts, and examples of parts of speech adorn the walls. A sign on the door reads, "The only place where success comes before work is in the dictionary."

Rachel offers me a chair in the back of the room, next to the wood stove that provides heat in winter. Suddenly the children enter. The girls wear brightly colored dresses of purple, turquoise, green, and blue, with their hair tucked under black caps. The boys wear bright shirts with suspenders and denim pants. Several of the children are barefoot; others wear sturdy black shoes.

Although no one talks, a feeling of excitement pervades the room as the children try not to stare at me. A few of the younger children, sitting in front, turn around to smile, their eyes round with curiosity.

The bustle of desk lids being raised and lowered gradually fades. Rachel calls the roll, asking the children to tell what chores they did before school this morning. "Fed the rabbits. Fed the chickens. Milked the cow. Fixed lunches. Wiped the dishes. Milked the goats" are a few of the replies.

Already, after only a few weeks of school, the routine is set—the teachers never have to remind the children what to do. Everyone stands and bows their heads for the Lord's Prayer. Rachel names two children, Justin and Mary Ann, to pass out hymnbooks and choose the songs for the day. Ruth offers one to me. The first song sets John 3:16 to the tune "Silent Night." I join in. Then we sing the beautifully haunting lyrics of "No Night There."

In the land of fadeless day
Lies a city foursquare.
It shall never pass away
And there is no night there.

All the gates with pearl are made,
In that city foursquare.
All the streets with gold are laid,
And there is no night there.

And the gates shall never close,
To that city foursquare.
There life's crystal river flows,
And there is no night there.

There they need no sunshine bright,
In that city foursquare.
For the Lamb is all the light,
And there is no night there.

Chorus:
God shall wipe away all tears
There's no death, no pain nor fears,
And they count no time by years,
And there is no night there.

After Rachel reads a Bible story and the children recite the Bible verse of the week (written on the board), lessons begin.

The teachers rely on each child to work independently at his or her seat while different grade levels take turns gathering at the teachers' tables for class. Whispering is not allowed. The children raise their hands if they need help.

"Sixth-grade arithmetic." Ruth calls the first group to her table in a voice so quiet that I can barely hear her. But the children understand her perfectly, and after a while, I tune in to her soft voice, too.

My friend David Yoder joins Orlie, Joseph, and Sadie at Ruth's table for sixth-grade math class. While they're correcting their workbooks and learning the next lesson, the children enjoy focused attention from the teacher. In these small groups, they freely ask questions, laugh at some of the answers, and speak up if they don't understand. When David gets one answer wrong, he politely defends his point, saying, "But this makes sense, too." Orlie and David seem to be good friends, and whenever David gets the right answer, Orlie grins and nods happily.

"Second-grade reading class." Ruth announces the next group in her soft, mild voice. The second graders have just finished reading a story at their seats, and now Ruth asks them comprehension questions, smiling gently when they get it right. When a child gives the wrong answer, she doesn't say, "no," but shakes her head almost imperceptibly and asks a further question to help the child remember.

While the children are reading the story aloud, Ruth nods at

Rachel Yoder, who patiently holds her hand up in the back of the room. "What does 'Arabic' mean?" Rachel asks. "Does that mean numbers?"

"It means the numbers we use," answers Ruth so quietly that the child in her reading group continues reading aloud without a break.

When it's time for morning recess, Rachel rings a bell. The children clear their desks. She softly says, "Stand," and the children file out in an orderly line.

At recess, Ruth offers me a plastic cup to use for drinking from the hand pump. The water tastes cool and fresh. The children use plastic cups to drink, or they jam one hand under the spout to force the water to spout through a hole in the top, creating a drinking fountain.

Out on the playground, handmade wooden swings, merry-go-round, and teeter-totter beckon the younger children. Ruth invites me to join a game of volleyball with the fifth through eighth graders. It's boys against girls, but to keep the numbers even, she joins the boys' side. The game is casual and lighthearted. When someone misses, teammates giggle. One time the ball hits me on the arm, and everyone laughs.

After recess, several children pull out jars filled with M&Ms and measure out a few to other scholars. Later Ruth tells me that a child must forfeit an M&M to anyone who hears them speaking German in the schoolyard. This game helps them to remember to speak only English, which they are supposed to learn in school. The first graders don't play the game, since most are learning English for the first time.

The rest of the morning passes with math and reading classes. When the lunch bell rings, the children stand and recite the blessing:

> Our hands we fold
> Our heads we bow
> Our food and drink
> We thank thee now.
> Amen.

Then they line up to wash their hands in a bowl of water at the dry sink in the cloakroom. The school has no running water and no bathroom, just a small outhouse next to the field.

At lunch time, I ask Ruth if there are any discipline problems, since the school is far more quiet and orderly than any I've ever seen. She smiles and says, "Oh yes!" As proof she shows me a sheet where she keeps a record of anytime when a child whispers while doing seatwork. If there are three offenses, the child has to stay in at recess and write a verse that's on the wall: "Study to be quiet and to do your own business and to work with your own hands." Only a few scattered checks appear on the sheet; the rest is blank.

Ruth suggests we carry a bench outside to sit on while we eat. The children cluster under the eaves of the building, eating out of their lunch boxes. The boys talk freely while they sit on the cement porch. The girls, bunched in the doorway close to me, self-consciously stop talking and try not to look at me curiously.

After lunch Ruth invites me to join a game, Broom Jail, with the younger children. It's a kind of a tag game, with several children being "It." Marilyn, a merry blond second grader, chases me relentlessly, laughing when she tags me.

A fleet-footed second grader named Justin finds it just as easy to catch me. After getting tagged three times, I become "It."

"I'm it!" I warn a solemn-looking first grader. She stares at me while I tag her, then scampers off to play on the swings. Later I realize that she probably hadn't learned English yet.

Lunch break over, the children listen to a Bible story. One girl crochets while a boy pastes colored paper on a collage. Then they settle into their afternoon studies: English, health, and history. By 2:30, some of the children have finished their assignments, and they select books from the little library. One of the eighth-grade girls named Rachel quizzes two second graders with addition flash cards, and the children race to call out the answer first in soft voices. My friend Grace Yoder reads a book for a few minutes and then quizzes some second graders with beautiful German script flash cards. Sadie and Robert help grade the fourth-graders' health workbooks.

By the end of the day, the children, though still working quietly in their seats, show signs of restlessness. A boy squeaks his desk lid up and down a few times. A few others smile at him, but he soon tires of making noise and goes back to his studies. When one boy comes back to his seat after health class, he rests for a moment on the desk of the girl who sits behind him. She gives his backside an exaggerated pinch, and he turns around and grins. Several children look at me and duck their heads, hiding their smiles shyly behind their hands. But 30 seconds later, they are back at work.

I realize suddenly that the school day has passed, and not once has either teacher used the words "no," "don't," or "shouldn't." Not once has a teacher reminded a child to be quiet or to do his or her work. Nor did the teachers praise the children or say, "good answer." With their gentle smiles, they quietly guided the students without disturbing their natural sense of dignity or self-sufficiency. Each child knew what to do and accomplished it quietly without much fuss or fear of failing.

At the end of the day, the Yoder children and I pile into the pony cart for the journey home, waving good-bye to several children in a buggy. Two tiny boys, dressed identically in light-colored shirts and dark suspenders, wait in an open buggy while their father talks on the community phone inside the schoolhouse. Their heads pop over the seat, straw hats bobbing as they smile and wave a final good-bye.

A letter from the Yoders, who helped me set up the school visit:

Thursday, May 19

Dear Linda,

Greetings sent to you from Bloomfield! We received your letter yesterday, and yes we still remember you. Yesterday was a nice warm day, and I mowed lawn all day long. Regina planted some more flowers and helped Mom work in the garden. I even got a *sunburn*.

About visiting that school, our school is out for this term. And I suppose you would have to ask the teacher and the board members. I don't know who our teacher will be for the next term. Guess we'll have to wait and see.

We have been very busy this spring already. My sister Darla married April 12. They had a big wedding. Then a grocery shower and then they moved to their new home. Do you remember where we turned around when I took you on your pony ride? That's the place they live on.

Next week I am invited to a wedding of my friends.

We have also helped my married sister Ruby and her husband Johnnie. They bought a farm to get it ready so they can move on it. I have to get this in the mailbox.

Bye

Annie and Regina Yoder

Excerpt from *The Budget:*

CROFTON, KY

NOV. 25—Merlin Beachy invited the Y.F.'s [young folks] and several families Wed. eve. to help on his woodworking shop, and the girls raked leaves in the yard.

A vanload from Ludington and Mio, Mich. areas stopped in at Ervin Beachys' for supper Wed. evening. They were enroute to Guthrie, Ky. to attend the wedding of Robert Yoder's daughter.

Last week one day a teacher and a home-schooling mother from Cadiz, Ky. came to visit our school. They were amazed and impressed by the order and discipline of our parochial schools, compared to the public schools.

note

1. John A. Hostetler and Gertrude Enders Huntington. *Children in an Amish Society*, pp. 91-92. Fort Worth, Indiana: Holt, Rinehart and Winston, Inc., 1971.

chapter

5

how Grace Yoder spent her summer vacation

In an Amish home, every child has a chore or job to do. The Amish believe that children should learn the satisfaction of a job well done at an early age. Industriousness is a virtue and a way of life. The Amish honor every job as important. Washing the clothes equals plowing the field or preaching a sermon.

During the school year, scholars might help feed the livestock, bring in the firewood, or mind the younger children after school. By helping out, every child feels needed and wanted.

Spring and summer are especially busy times for the Amish. Like country schools a century ago, Amish schools let out a month early so children can help with planting and other farmwork.

There's also time for summer fun—reading, climbing trees, and going on picnics. Sometimes the Yoder family drives their horse and buggy to a nearby lake for a day of food, fishing, and visiting with their aunts, uncles, and cousins. And with so many brothers and sisters around, there's always someone to share work or play.

Grace Yoder doesn't have time to get bored during summer vacation, even though it's four months long. Since the beginning of May, when her Amish school finished classes for the year, she has been busy helping her mother and sisters tend the garden, prepare meals, milk cows, mow the lawn, and care for her baby brother, Wayne.

"Right when I sat up in bed this morning I went out and helped milk the cows," says Grace. That was at 6:00 a.m. After breakfast, she started mowing the lawn "and that took most of the forenoon. After dinner, I helped do the dishes and fold the laundry. That's about it."

Right now it's 2:30 on a sunny Friday afternoon, and I'm helping her load grass clippings into a bucket to spread under the strawberry plants. Already, by the third of June, the berries hang swollen under the leaves, plump and red.

What do the grass clippings do?

"Oh, they keep the ground moist," says Grace. "And help with the weeds."

She's barefoot, and she says it feels good. I take my shoes off, too. My feet sink into the rich earth, cool and soft. It's a huge garden, with neat rows of potatoes, peas, onions, radishes, lettuce, tomatoes, beans, and sweet corn stretching for what must be a quarter of an acre. And of course, strawberries.

There's not a weed in sight. Last Tuesday Grace and her older sisters hoed the ground between the plants.

Grace speaks politely with a shy, slow smile. She wears a navy-blue dress and white apron, with a light aqua scarf, folded like a bonnet, to cover her dark hair. She'll turn 13 this summer and will enter the eighth grade next year.

Her teacher just got married last week. As we carry another bucket of soft grass clippings to the garden, Grace tells me about the wedding. It took place on a Thursday, as do most weddings in her community. Grace visited with many of her friends, since most of the older scholars were there. After church and a ceremony at a neighbor's home, the bride's parents served dinner at their house. Mostly Grace and her friends sat around and talked after dinner, but in the evening the young people played volleyball.

The mulching finished, we visit the new baby chicks in the tidy wooden chicken house. It's Grace's job to feed them each evening before she helps her sister Annie milk three of the family's cows— Vera, Jolean, and Pam.

"Then I come in and just watch the baby or something like that. After dinner we wash the dishes and go to bed."

When she's not baby-sitting Wayne or helping with chores, Grace likes to read. The whole family takes an hour after the noon meal to lie down and rest. "I like to read about old times, when the Indians were still here, and Westerns, too." She also climbs trees ("to see how high I can get") and plays outdoors with her younger brothers or goes fishing with them.

Does she miss seeing her friends, now that school is out?

"I see them at church," she says. And sometimes a family comes over for a Sunday meal, and the young people visit then.

Back at the garden, Nancy, Grace's mother, picks strawberries while four-year-old Leah entertains baby Wayne. A chubby, healthy looking child, he sits up straight on the lawn near his mother. A blue cap covers his head.

Grace's lively sister, Regina, walks over to chat. She spent the morning washing the family's laundry, hanging it on a clothesline to dry, and folding it. Her older sister Annie is busy mowing the rest of the lawn right now. Regina says that the whole family traveled in a van to their grandparent's farm in northern Iowa last weekend for a Yoder family reunion. More than 200 relatives came from Illinois, Indiana, and Iowa.

How did they spend the time?

"Oh, we just caught up on a lot of visiting," says Regina.

Just then we see the pony prancing down the road, tugging Grace's father and younger brothers in the pony cart, shiny yellow fishing rods flashing in the sun.

Smiling, Nancy says, "The boys were so excited about their new fishing poles. The night after they got them, they both dreamed that they went fishing and some other boys took their poles home by mistake!" She says that often they catch 17 bass, enough for the whole family to eat.

Nancy quietly asks Grace to take Wayne out of the sun. "Grace is my baby-sitter," says Nancy appreciatively.

As Grace and I walk to the shady tree in front of the house, she says that Wayne is the happiest baby of all the children. Her mother thinks it's because he has so many brothers and sisters to hold him. Grace settles on the swing by the driveway. Wayne, safe in her lap, grabs at the metal chain.

I greet Toby, Grace's father. They caught no fish today. Toby suspects it's because the recent rains churned up the water, leaving it muddy.

After Robert leads the pony to the barn, he and David join me at the picnic table. Suddenly, the sound of bleating spikes the air.

"The sheep are out!" cries Robert. The two boys race across the barnyard, bare feet flying over mud. They chase the sheep back through the gate, fastening it securely. A minute later the boys stroll back to the picnic table to chat with me.

Robert and David, who are now eight and 11, spend most of their summer days together, helping their father care for the sows, sheep, and horses. On the days when their father uses farm machinery to mow hay or plant fields, they can't help with "all that big stuff," says David. So they have time to go fishing, play with their trucks in the sandbox, or ride Midnight the pony around the pasture.

"If it's a nice day and the birds are singing, I like to ride slow," says David. "Otherwise, I like to go for it." When David smiles, his eyes gleam playfully.

On rainy days the boys play in the barn— "You know, when you can hear the rain beatin' on the roof," says David. Occasionally the two brothers ride the pony out to the fields to watch their father mow hay. There they try to save pheasant and possum nests that accidentally get disturbed in the mowing.

We walk over to the shed to see the new colt, only one day old. She's the offspring of Sidney, the Percheron mare owned by their older brother, Dan. The colt's hair sticks out rough and fuzzy, and she nuzzles her mother.

"I was hoping we could name her Flicka," says David wistfully.

"But it's Dan's horse, so he'll probably name her," says Grace in her big-sister voice.

It's around 4:30 p.m., time for evening chores. Back at the barn, Annie and Regina sing as they milk the cows. Grace helps Annie milk the gentle and easy cow named Vera.

The boys use a coffee can to measure oats for each horse stall. They know exactly which stall each horse and colt will feed in. This is important, because the colts don't eat the vitamins, Superfoot feed, and soybean meal that grown horses do.

Suddenly the air fills with warm smells of hair and sweat. Five mares—followed by newborn colts Vicki, Challenger, Princess, Dixie, and Babe—trot into the barn. Toby slips halters on the colts, and the two boys fasten the horses. Little Leah holds a straw out to Babe, hoping the colt will eat it.

The horses fed, we head over to the rabbit cages to water and feed them. The boys own 22 rabbits. They raise them as pets and to sell. Robert stops to get a bucket of water from the hydrant by the street, since the rabbits like cold water.

David says, "You have to pet them or they act just like wild rabbits. My brother Dan raised rabbits, and he put them up in the hay mow. Of course they had lots of babies. You'd go up there and all you'd see is tails disappearing. You couldn't find one rabbit when you tried to catch them. He sold them the next spring. He was done with them."

David and Robert's rabbits live in large cages shaded by trees. The boys change their water and feed them oats and hay twice a day.

David pulls a brown baby rabbit out of the cage. "This is my favorite one, because he's so cuddly. Want to hold him?"

Soft and sleek, the rabbit snuggles against my stomach while I stroke it. "Do you remember to do your chores every day, or does someone have to remind you?" I ask.

"The clock reminds you that it's time," says David. "I used to forget sometimes. You know, if you aren't used to it and just go play after helping Dad with the horses."

As a favorite summer treat, their father takes them to auctions at the sale barn. "There are lots of little animals there—lambs and baby pigs—and, you know, all those animals make a lot of noise!" says David, his eyes bright with excitement. The auctioneer takes bids on their rabbits, and they sell well.

"Dad saves the money for us until we get older," explains Robert.

I wave good-bye to Grace, David, and Robert, their chores finished for the day. As I drive away, Robert scoots his new wooden wagon, a gift from last Christmas, across the yard to watch the animals leaving the barn for the night.

an Amish author

Bloomfield, Iowa, is also the home of David Wagler, an author well known in Amish circles. Besides writing books and running his own press and mail-order bookstore, he has served as a correspondent for *The Budget* for over 50 years. Unlike other *Budget* correspondents, though, David is famous for sharing more than the births, deaths, and happenings of his Amish community. When he runs across some useful information in his travels or readings, he likes to share it with his Amish brethren. Unfortunately, due to space constraints, much of this fascinating extra material gets cut. Undaunted, David decided to collect all of his unpublished out-takes in his much-loved book, *Stories Behind the News.*

Here's a David Wagler column that didn't get cut from *The Budget.*

Sept. 20—Our church services were at Leo Yoders' and to be at Marvin Troyers' next time. Marie Yoder from Ludington, Mich. attended as she has been helping her brother here for some time.

My cousin, Mahlon, and wife, Mary (Yoder) Wagler, from Hutchinson, Ks. had dinner with us on Friday. They were on their way to a reunion in Indiana.

Norman and Ida Yutzy are having a big close-out sale on Saturday, Oct. 16th starting at 9:30. I understand they have a good selection of valuable merchandise which has been collected over the years. Elmer's will be taking over the operation of the farm.

Recently I read the article entitled "A City on a Hill" which is in the summer 1993 issue of *Small Farmers Journal*. The subtitle of the article is "Some Thoughts on the Book After The Fire, the Destruction of the Lancaster County Amish." The author of the article is "Uncle Amos" and it so happens that he is an Amishman. It is the most thought-provoking article I have read for a long, long time and enough to cause anyone to lose some sleep over. It is about the tourist business in Lancaster county. The author likens it to a Trojan horse and said it was a fine-looking animal when it first made its appearance in the '50s, prancing up and down main street and bringing in a lot of money for local merchants. But the beautiful horse turned into a different creature after he opened the flood gates which brought the 5 million tourists every year. Many of these have decided to stay in this "peaceful environment," buying a home right next to the Amish farmer with his assortment of cows, hogs and chickens with all the odors which go with such a business. Then suddenly there is a clash of values of the simple rural people against the flood of outsiders who do not hold the same ideas. When smelly cows become an affront to sophisticated nostrils and sweating horses are viewed as cruelty to animals the residents of the area suddenly change from a quaint people to backward, stupid and a traffic hazard.

The author throws out a challenge by asking, "Are we a national treasure? Do we have a right to be preserved?" He says the answer is an emphatic "No" and if we are to survive it must be through the faith and religious dedication which took us over the past centuries. He says the church was able to endure persecution but he is not at all sure it can survive the continual limelight. He also cites incidents which pose the question, "Whose values are being absorbed?" He says many non-Amish wish they had our values but are not willing to work at acquiring and keeping them. They think we are what we are because of our way of life. But they have the cart before the horse because the truth is we live our way of life because of what we are. If it is something that will survive it must come from the inside out.

I am anxious to contact "Uncle Amos" as I have some questions I would very much like to ask him. I have reason to believe he reads *The Budget*, so if you read this, please send me your name and address to Rt. 8, Bloomfield, Iowa 52537. It will be kept strictly confidential, but please do write. David Wagler.

chapter

6

snaps, buckles, and straps

*E*ven though most Amish people still live on farms, more young people today must make their living in other ways because of the rising prices of farmland. They may make furniture, buggies, or harnesses. Some Amish even work in factories. These trades involving manual labor are permitted by the church, because a man can still work with his hands or "by the sweat of his brow."

Once their eight years of formal schooling end, young people start their vocational training, learning the occupations of their parents. From their mothers, teenage girls learn how to raise garden vegetables, sew their own clothes, and prepare home-cooked meals. Teenage boys learn farming skills or a trade from their fathers.

The Amish consider this apprenticeship to be an essential part of a young person's education and the best way to prepare for a

51

successful life in the Amish community. Teenagers learn to work with steady focus and efficiency, which is the Amish way. "We don't care whose time it is, we just don't like to waste it," as one Amish man put it. The Amish are known as reliable and careful craftsmen.

Even though electricity is not used in the home and on the farm, many Amish communities allow carpenters to use drills, saws, and other power tools on the job. Amish businesses must still operate without a telephone, though.

Even if an Amish family runs a grocery store or harness shop, like the family in this story, they would probably still own an "acreage" or small farm to raise cash crops, chickens, cows, horses, and vegetables. That way, the children could still learn enough farming skills to run their own farm someday, which is the desire of most Amish people. In the meantime, the family could raise most of its own food.

I t's a central part of every Amish community. The neighborhood harness shop is where farmers take their leather harnesses to be cleaned, oiled, and repaired. It's also the place where a young man can buy a shiny new harness for his first horse and buggy.

Jonathan looks forward to making his own harness soon. At 16, he spends his days working side by side with his father in the family's harness shop just off a gravel road in Iowa.

Today Jonathan stands at a tall machine called a riveter, punching shiny silver rivets into leather straps. Dye the same color as his black hair stains his hands.

"I've been doing a lot of dyeing the last few days," he says, shyly smiling.

Does it come off?

"Oh yeah, Mom thinks so. Kinda takes a while."

Jonathan no longer attends the one-room Amish school down the road, having completed his formal education with eighth grade. During the past two years he has learned the trade of his father—

cutting, trimming, dyeing, sewing, riveting, and assembling the leather harnesses that Amish farmers use on their huge Belgian and Percheron workhorses to pull wagons and plows.

But when I comment on his skills, he smiles and says, "I suppose other people know things about farming that I don't know." Because he and his father spend their days in the shop, they operate only a small farm of 35 acres, growing soybeans and other cash crops. There's also a vast vegetable garden behind the house, where Jonathan's mother and sister Ada, 13, raise the family's food.

Jonathan's father, Rudy, built the shop himself three years ago, along with the large white house it's attached to. The smell of raw leather and dye hangs in the air. Huge sheets of leather, loosely rolled like giant cinnamon sticks, pour out of shelves at the rear of the shop. Harnesses and bridles loop from ceiling hooks. Hundreds of buckles and snaps, rings and rivets nestle in open-faced boxes that line up neatly on wooden shelves. One entire wall is for silver-colored parts, the other for golden-colored parts. Bits and scraps lap the cement floor like a collage—thin spaghetti noodles, triangles, squares, and dots.

While most of the machines in the shop work by leverage and involve no power, two oversized sewing machines run by an air compressor stitch leather straps together. The air compressor can be switched on for short intervals, leaving the shop free of machine noise most of the time.

How did Rudy learn the trade?

"I used to tell people I learned from mistakes," he says. He's easy to talk to, with his pleasant laugh and ready jokes. His smile peeks through a reddish beard and his bangs are cropped straight across the forehead. "My Dad had a repair shop. He never made new stuff."

The larger share of their business goes to "English" people who buy workhorses for fairs and amusement parks and to others who purchase a horse for the first time and need a bridle and harness.

"This summer we already have shipped from Massachusetts to California," says Rudy as he hammers a hole in a leather strap. He's never advertised, attracting all of his orders from repeat business or by word of mouth. "They say more people use horses now than back when people used horses."

Jonathan shows me how to use one of the hundreds of tools in the shop, which spill out of round wooden holders above the wide workbench. Most of the tools are handmade, with smooth, wooden handles that fit the curve of the palm. Nails, screws, and washers glisten in separate compartments of a metal plate, like shiny candies in a candy dish.

Just assembling a harness is a complicated business. It involves dozens of snaps, buckles, and straps, all connected in a particular way.

"See that hame strap I made a bit ago?" asks Jonathan. He starts building a new harness from the straps they've made this morning. "It holds together these two hames." He explains that a hame is the stiff piece that fits over the collar of the harness.

I'm already confused, so Rudy shows me a photo album filled with snapshots from customers of horses wearing his completed harnesses. He points out all the different parts: bridle, collar, hames, breast strap, breaching, hip straps, back pad, tugs, driving lines. (See Figure 1.)

Rudy flips the photo album to the next page. "Now these are the big guys—only 30 inches tall," he jokes. It takes me a minute to figure it out. It's a photo of two miniature horses outfitted in complete miniature harnesses and pulling a miniature wagon.

Meanwhile, Jonathan connects the breast strap to a huge three-way snap that requires some fancy looping. In and out his hand weaves, neatly tucking the strap in at the end.

"Yeah, that took me a while to get figured out," says Jonathan. "But I've done it lots and lots of times already now."

A while later Jonathan displays the finished harness, hanging on the harness rack. It's huge and much too heavy for me to pick up. Now I can see why some people opt for the lighter-weight plastic kind, even though they don't last nearly as long.

Jonathan steps over a pile of dirty leather straps and buckles. "These are some harnesses people brought in to get cleaned," he says. "If they take good care of them, they pretty well last forever."

How often do farmers bring them in to get cleaned and oiled?

"Some of 'em, not often enough," says Rudy with a laugh. "Once a year, we aim at."

"That's usually my job," says Jonathan with a rueful smile. "Dirty one like this, I'll probably put in a tub with warm water and soap—we've got saddle soap—and just wash it off and scrub it. Sometimes if it's not too bad, I don't need to put it in water. I'll just scrub it."

Jonathan shows me a huge oval metal tub, bigger than a bathtub, filled with neat's-foot oil, a pale yellow, odorless oil made from cow's bones. Above it, looped on a giant hook, dangle the endless straps and buckles of an old harness, drying out after a dip in the oil. The straps feel soft and oily.

A truck pulls into the driveway, and an older man and his son amble in, carrying a worn-out saddle that they want refurbished. "I told my boys you were the man to do it," says the older man.

Rudy laughs and says, "I guess we'll try to give it a good going over." He writes up the order at his desk. A copy of *Harness Shop News* (a trade journal containing industry news, notes, and advertisements) rests on top of a pile of papers. The back cover reads, "Your Business, your horse/Don't feed 'em, they're gonna die!/Advertising is food for your business—don't let it starve/Call the *Harness Shop News* Today!" An outdated cover of the 1993 Mule Calendar, showing a team in full harness, hangs on the wall beside him.

"We can drop you a card when we're done," says Rudy. "That way you won't have to drive out."

The younger man inspects the ready-made halters that hang along one wall of the shop, ducking under bundles of multicolored lead-ropes streaming from the ceiling like rainbows. He buys a red halter for his colt.

How many customers come to their shop each day? "We've had days here where one or two come, other days a lot more," says Rudy. "On a horse sale day down here in town, we'll maybe get 30 customers. They buy a horse and then they need a harness."

Another truck and a van drive in. One farmer jokes with Rudy; another tells a story about riding a horse to school and being chased by a giant runaway sow.

Around 4:00 p.m., Jonathan uses a torch to ignite the gas light above the workbench, filling the darkening room with warm, golden light. Jonathan's younger brothers troop in, eyes and faces bright from the long hike home from school in the cold winter air. They exchange their muddy boots for indoor shoes at the back of the shop.

Floyd, age 12, and Samuel, age eight, say they usually help fasten buckles on the leather straps and sometimes they dye the edges. Today there's little for them to do in the shop, so they head outside to do their chores, feeding the chickens and peacocks and carrying in wood.

As I say good-bye, Jonathan is riveting more straps and Rudy is threading a needle and handsewing a decorative leather collar. There will be a break for dinner, then they will work in the shop until 8:00 to keep up with the orders.

Will Jonathan be making the harness for his first horse and buggy this year?

"I hope so," he says with his quiet smile. "Maybe this winter."

---

how to make a harness

1. **Cut**. First Rudy and Jonathan choose the leather, which comes in natural cinnamon-brown or pre-dyed black. Then Rudy cuts the shape they need, snipping curved shapes with scissors and slicing straight lines with a tool that is held like a knife but has a razor at the tip.

2. **Trim**. Jonathan trims the edges with a sharp tool, stripping off spaghetti-thin strands of leather, leaving a smoother, rounder edge. Selecting another tool that looks like the point of a triangle, he shapes the end of the strap into a point.

3. **Dye**. Jonathan opens a jar of dye and brushes it onto the edges with a paintbrush so the newly cut edges match the rest of the strap.

4. **Mark**. Next he threads the strap through a machine that presses grooves into the edges of the straps. These serve as guidelines if any stitching is needed, or as decoration.
5. **Sew**. If the strap needs to be particularly strong (such as the "tugs" that connect the horse to the wagon), Jonathan stitches two straps together with one of the two oversized standing sewing machines.
6. **Add buckles or snaps**. Jonathan chooses a buckle or snap to match the size of the strap and attaches it to the end.
7. **Rivet**. Jonathan uses the riveting machine to press a metal rivet into the strap, which has been looped back to keep the buckle or snap in place.
8. **Decorate**. For their non-Amish customers, Rudy adds shiny metal "dots" for decoration. The Amish harnesses stay plain black.
9. **Assemble**. Jonathan connects the dozens of straps, buckles, and snaps into a finished harness.

(See pages 58 and 59.)

parts of a harness   figure 1a

driving harness

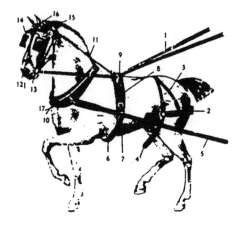

1 lines	6 belly band	12 front overcheck
2 breeching	7 shaft loop	13 blinds
3 hip stap	8 bearer	14 winker stay
4 hold back	9 gig saddle	15 crown
5 trace	10 hame strap	16 brow band
	11 rein	17 hames

draft harness

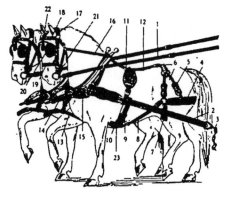

1 lines	9 billet	17 crown
2 traces	10 market strap	18 brow band
3 heel chain	11 back pad	19 nose band
4 breeching	12 back strap	20 blinds
5 safe	13 choke stap	21 throat latch
6 hip strap	14 breast strap	22 face drop
7 lazy strap	15 hames	23 belly band
8 quarter strap	16 reins	

part three

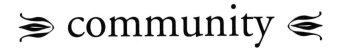 community

chapter

7

the heart of Amish life

*T*he Amish do not build churches
for worship. They take turns holding the services in their large
homes. Usually 30 or 40 families make up one church district—
and they live close enough together so they can travel to church in a
horse and buggy.

Having church in the home requires a remarkable amount of
organization. The Amish usually build their homes with removable
walls to create a large space on the first floor. When a family's turn
comes up, the closest neighbors help clean the house, prepare the food,
set up and take down the benches and tables, and serve the food.

Singing plays an important role in the Amish service. Since the
Amish do not use musical instruments, they sing their church hymns
without accompaniment. The Amish rely on the Ausbund—the
oldest Protestant hymnal in use—containing the German text for

140 hymns but no musical notes. The tunes have been handed down by memory from generation to generation.

Young men learn how to "lead" each song, singing the first few words of each line solo. It takes a great deal of skill, because the leader must sing perfectly on pitch without a cue from an instrument. Also, because High German is the language for hymns and Bible readings, young Amish men and women must attend "German school" in order to learn how to read the words of the songs and Bible verses. High German differs from the vernacular Pennsylvania German spoken in Amish homes and used for the sermons, testimonies, and announcements at church.

A bishop, a deacon, and one or two ministers govern each church district. The Amish do not elect their church officials; they nominate several responsible men and make the final choice by lottery. Once chosen, a man holds the position for life. The Amish do not consider it particularly lucky to be selected, since the position includes heavy responsibilities. In addition to making a normal living, a minister must spend many hours preparing and memorizing sermons, with no compensation for his time.

While the bishop and ministers must be male, the entire community (men and women) vote on major issues, deciding the strict rules of daily life (Ordnung) based on scripture. If a problem comes up, church members stay behind after the Sunday service to discuss and vote on the issue.

The Amish go to church every second Sunday. On the Sundays off, they usually visit relatives or friends, or in warmer months, the whole family attends Sunday school together. After Sunday school, they return home for dinner, go visiting, or have company.

One mother told me she sometimes invites two or three families after church, which means that she and her daughters prepare food for 30 to 40 people. A typical meal for guests on Sunday might be meatloaf, mashed potatoes, Jello salad, and cake, fruit, or pie.

When they don't have guests, the family eats lightly to give the women a rest from cooking. Favorite Sunday evening meals include popcorn, pizza, and ice cream.

Nettie looks forward to Sunday as a day of rest, a day to worship, and a day to visit with her friends. For her Amish family, preparations for Sunday worship start the day before. On Saturday afternoon 11-year-old Nettie and her sisters bathe, wash and braid their hair, and iron their Sunday clothes. In warm weather, they wash the black buggies the family will drive to church. Nettie fills the wood bin with enough wood to last until Monday, and her 13-year-old sister, Ada, helps bake cakes and bread so Sunday meals will be simple to make.

"Saturday is always a special day for me," says Freda, Nettie's mother, "because we prepare ourselves for the Sabbath, the day of rest."

One Sunday in March I board a black Amish buggy with Nettie, her parents, and her younger sister and brother, Joanna and Jonas. Nettie's older brothers and sisters ride in a second buggy.

Although the horses, Comet and Ranger, trot at a slow pace, it's hard to hear each other speak above the roar of gravel flying and wheels spinning. Another buggy pulls in front of us.

"That's my brother Harley and his family," calls out Nettie's father, Cephas, above the roar. A while later, Cephas points out his nephew Marcus and his wife, newly married last summer, walking up a crossroad in their Sunday best. Everyone on the road, it seems, flows to the same destination—the large white farmhouse of the Beachy family in Kalona, Iowa, where church will be held this morning.

Black buggies crowd the yard when we arrive. The white wooden church wagon, which transports the benches, songbooks, and dishes from house to house, sits on the side lawn.

Nettie, Freda, Joanna, and I walk inside, where a group of women stand quietly in the glassed-in porch. Nettie and Freda neatly fold their black shawls and lay them on a long table along with their black bonnets.

As each woman enters, Freda greets her with a handshake and a kiss. Freda tells me it's called the kiss of fraternal love, exchanged between church members of the same gender. Each woman greets me with a handshake and a kind smile, and I feel truly welcomed. There's a reverent feeling and very little conversation, but it's a warm kind of quiet.

I notice that the men and small boys gather in the living room but do not mix with the women. Joanna, like other preschool girls, clings to her mother's skirt. Nettie and her sister Ada talk quietly with their school-age friends under a tree outside. The school-age boys wait in the basement.

There seem to be about twice as many women as men. After we seat ourselves on backless benches facing the men's section, Bishop Yoder and the ministers cross to the women's side to greet us with a handshake.

As the clock ticks closer to 9:30 a.m., a thick blanket of silence covers the room. School-age boys file in silently from the basement, and then the girls, who sit on benches right behind me. Preschool girls sit with their mothers, boys (and some girls if their mothers are sick) sit with their fathers.

I once read about the a cappella singing at Amish services, but nothing prepares me for its beauty. Somewhere between a song and a chant, voices rise and swell in unison, slowly spinning out each syllable in a sustained phrase of five or 10 notes. The men's and women's voices blend into a beautiful pattern, the men sometimes holding a note to create an effect like an organ or drone.

At first I'm not used to the slow pace. I keep thinking it must be time to turn the page, but I finally figure out that it can take 15 or 20 minutes to sing a one-page song of four verses. At once mournful and joyous, a dirge and melody, the hymn fills my heart with devotion.

Standing between the men's and women's sections, the first minister begins his talk. His voice rises and falls in the lilting rhythms of a gifted speaker. Even though I don't understand the Pennsylvania German language, I can hear the poetry in his words. At one point, everyone turns completely around. Facing the back of the room, we kneel to pray in front of our benches.

Another round of singing ends the service. I can't believe we've been sitting there for three hours, with only a few wails from the babies, who for the most part lay contentedly in their mothers' arms. Preschoolers such as Joanna must stay completely silent throughout the service, although when Joanna grew tired of sitting on the backless bench, she rested her head in her mother's lap.

The schoolgirls file out again, and the rest of us stand chatting while a group of men efficiently clear away the benches. They set up one long table for the men and another long table for the women. In just a few minutes Freda guides me to the table for the first serving, usually reserved for the elderly and guests like me. The room suddenly grows quiet as we bow our heads in silent prayer before the meal.

Heaping plates of sliced homemade bread, egg salad spread, "Amish" peanut butter (peanut butter mixed with honey), homemade apple butter, sweet dill pickles, and pickled beets are set within easy reach of each diner. The Amish purposely keep the shared Sunday meals simple and ritually the same so the women do not have to work too hard. A server comes around with refills of mint tea and water.

I've eaten three sandwiches and am chatting with Freda when a hush steals over the room. We offer another silent thanks; the Amish pray before and after every meal.

While another group sits to eat, women stand or sit in small groups around the room, talking amiably. I am never left alone—a stream of friendly women make me feel at home throughout the afternoon. Sturdy preschoolers toddle about the room, dressed in dark blue pants and suspenders like their fathers or long dresses and black prayer caps like their mothers. A smiling teenage girl named Martha Beachy lets me hold her hefty baby cousin, who is wrapped in layers of pink blankets and is also named Martha Beachy.

The afternoon passes quickly. All the time we're visiting, the Beachys and their team of helpers have been working steadily, serving tables and cleaning up. Now they rest and share homemade banana cream pies brought by another family to treat the servers. Because I'm a guest, I'm offered a piece, too.

It's 3:00 by the time we finally start home, one of the last families to leave. In the buggy, I learn that Nettie and her friends spent the afternoon looking at scrapbooks and talking in the nearby trailer of Mrs. Susie Miller (an elder member of the church who rents from the Beachys since her husband died). Jonas and other young boys played games in the basement. Ada visited with the other girls in the trailer for a while, then rode home early with her older brothers and sisters.

By the time we arrive at the farm, there's just a short time left before evening chores and a light supper of toasted cheese sandwiches, soup, and hot chocolate. A large bowl of popcorn sits on the counter, a favorite Sunday afternoon snack. For Nettie and her family, this truly has been "a day to forget your weekly cares."

At every service, the well-known hymn "Das Lob Lied" is sung in its original German before the ministers speak. It was written by Leonhard Klock in both German and Dutch, and it first appeared in the third edition of the book of hymns called the *Ausbund* in 1622. Some communities take 30 minutes to sing it, others only 20.

Das Lob Lied
(the hymn of praise)[1]

1. O Lord Father, we bless thy name,
Thy love and thy goodness praise;
That thou, O Lord, so graciously
Have been to us always.
Thou hast brought us together, O Lord,
To be admonished through thy word.
Bestow on us thy grace.

2. O may thy servant be endowed
With wisdom from on high,
To preach thy word with truth and power,

Thy name to glorify.
Which needful is to thy own praise,
Give hunger for thy word always,
This should be our desire.

3. Put wisdom in our hearts while here
On earth thy will be known,
Thy word through grace to understand
What thou would have us to do.
To live in righteousness, O Lord,
Submissive to thy word,
That all our vows prove true.

4. Thine only be the glory, O Lord,
Likeness all might and power.
That we praise thee in our assembly
And feel grateful every hour.
With all our hearts we pray,
Wilt thou be with us every day
Through Christ our Lord. Amen.

✳

nicknaming among the Amish

Because all the Amish in America have descended
from a handful of families, there are less than 50 last
names in the entire Amish population. This proves
especially confusing when two children from different families have the same last name and the same
Christian name. To avoid mix-ups, the Amish refer
to each other with nicknames.

Usually humorous or even unflattering, the
nicknames may be about an event in a person's life.
Joe Wittmer, who grew up in an Amish family, says
that his family was called "Dixie" because one of his

forefathers bought a farm from a family with that name. He cites other nicknames such as "Bottle," "Turkey," and "Hey-Hey."[2] John Beiler, who translated the "Lob Lied" into English (see above) was nicknamed "Mechanicsburg" John because he lived nearer to Mechanicsburg than another Lancaster County man named John Beiler. Another famous Beiler was called "Rhyming" Aaron Beiler (b. 1881) because he had the habit of speaking in rhymes.[3]

No Amish people ever refer to themselves by their nicknames, although they are certainly aware of what others call them. It's all part of the good-natured teasing that takes place in a close-knit community, and it does serve a necessary purpose.

notes

1. This English translation was made by John Beiler in 1933. David Luthy, "Beiler/Byler Family History," *Family Life* (May 1995): 19-20. Reprinted with permission from Pathway Publications, Aylmer, Ontario.

2. Joe Wittmer, *The Gentle People: Personal Reflections of Amish Life*, pp. 59-60. Minneapolis, Minnesota: Educational Media Corporation, 1991.

3. David Luthy, "Beiler/Byler Family History," *Family Life* (May 1995): 19-20.

8

quilting above Stringtown Grocery

*T*he Amish believe that Christian ideals such as "help thy neighbor" should be practiced in daily life. Because they help each other in emergencies, they do not buy fire or health insurance. They also do not take any government aid and do not pay social security taxes.

No one in need gets forgotten. After the Amish church service I attended in Kalona, a woman cut up a calendar and gave one date to each person. She explained that this system ensured that an elderly church member with cancer would receive a visit, a meal, or a letter every day of the month.

If a farmer's barn burns down, the entire community gathers to rebuild the barn. But rather than being a chore, these community gatherings are called "frolics." The women and girls prepare a feast, and the men and boys raise the barn in a single day. Everyone looks *forward to frolics as a chance to break the routine and see their friends.*

Some work parties are attended by "young folks" (teenagers) only. I was once invited to a wood-stacking party, where the young folks of Bloomfield spent one Friday evening helping a sick neighbor store wood for the winter.

Children look forward to apple snitzing, a festive fall event when neighbors gather to make apple cider at a community press. Amish farmers share their farmwork and their equipment as well, forming "rings" that travel from farm to farm to thresh grain or fill silos. "Work that can be done by one is more enjoyable when shared" is the Amish belief.

The Amish also give generously to their non-Amish neighbors. Monroe Herschberger and his construction team rebuilt a neighbor's house destroyed by fire—for free. When Hurricane Hugo swept away whole towns in South Carolina, the Amish arrived with other volunteers to help rebuild.

"The men and boys would work all day building houses, the women would cook us meals, and the teenage girls minded my children and got them to laugh again," recalls a grateful survivor. "They slept on the floor or in tents outside for weeks."

Amish women are famous for their colorful homemade quilts, which they often finish off in a group "sewing." Besides making quilts for their families and relatives, most Amish communities hold a monthly sewing to stitch quilts for needy people around the world. The women look forward to the sewings as a chance to visit.

I hear the squeal of small children as I climb the wooden stairs to the spacious room above the String-town Grocery in Kalona one October day. The wooden floors and wide windows make it a cheerful place to work. Amish women group around six large quilting frames, their dark, plain clothing contrasting with the colors of the quilts. The soft patter of women's voices mingles with the children's laughter.

Leona, the spry, gray-haired woman who invited me, stands up to greet me. As one of several elected women, she helps organize these sewings every six weeks. Leona and her sister Mary also make finely crafted quilts for "English" buyers.

Each quilt in the room today displays a different pattern. I'm dazzled by Lone Star, a quilt made of tiny blue and pink squares, which is adorned with a pink border carefully stitched with flowers, stars, and four-leaf clovers in the tiniest stitches imaginable. Leona tells me that these traditional Amish designs have been passed down for generations.

Leona introduces me to Sarah and Rosanna, two friends who graduated from eighth grade last spring at age 15. Now they spend their days learning how to run a household by helping their mothers at home.

Sarah's slender, long arms come in handy while stretching across the quilt. Her gentle eyes, framed by glasses, welcome me. She ducks her head and smiles endearingly when she speaks.

Rosanna wears a brown cape over a brown dress. Beautiful blond hair peeks from her prayer cap, her gaze steady and serious. They share the frame with three other teenage girls—Miriam, Marietta, and Eunice. Dorothy, a newly married woman with smooth pink cheeks, completes the group.

Someone offers me a folding chair and the girls scoot over to make room for me. I like the quilt's bright green and red calico pattern. It lies flat like a tablecloth on a square table, except there's no wood under the cloth, just a wooden frame around the edges. Stretched taut and clamped securely at the ends of the frame, the cloth can't slide around when you sew. The girls sit in chairs around the sides, bending over it to make the hundreds of tiny stitches that hold the layers of the quilt together.

The women sew the quilts for needy people in other countries. "A lot of our quilts go to Haiti," says Leona, who stands by my chair helping me get comfortable. "Not for warmth, but to put on the floor and use as a bed."

"Your quilt design is called Boston Commons," she says. Its rectangular design does look like the green lawn called "commons."

I've never quilted before, so Dorothy lends me her thimble and shows me how to stitch. Watching her, it looks so simple. But when I try it, the needle gets stuck. I notice how big my stitches are compared to Sarah's and Rosanna's, but Dorothy soothingly says, "Practice makes perfect."

The girls certainly do get a lot of practice at these sewings. Both Sarah and Rosanna arrived around 10:00 and will stay until 4:00. They first started attending sewings a few years ago during school holidays, and now they come regularly.

Sarah started sewing by hand around age nine or 10, but she doesn't remember when she first sewed by machine. "I think I tried before I was supposed to," she says. Everyone laughs.

"That's when we like doing it most," says Dorothy.

Have they made their own quilts at home?

Dorothy made her first quilt at 16. She says that most women make quilts later in life, for their married children.

"I pieced a quilt for my bed when I was 13 or 14," says Rosanna, "but it isn't really my quilt." Sarah says she pieced a nine-patch to cover a tear in an old quilt. Both girls help their mothers do handsewing, such as the hems on dresses or pants. Sarah says she sews simple things, including handkerchiefs, on the sewing machine.

Sarah and Rosanna giggle when Sarah's needle gets stuck. "This stitch is so big—there's something lumpy under here," says Sarah.

A little after noon, a woman on the other side of the room starts a song, and everyone joins in. It's in German, so I can't understand the words, but I can enjoy the lilting voices. After the last words fade away, everyone stands with their arms folded across their chests, heads bowed, reciting in German.

"That's the Lord's Prayer in German," explains Dorothy.

And the song?

"It's a blessing that we sing at each sewing before the meal."

The blessings for the meal over, everyone moves to chairs along the side of the room and eats lunch out of plastic containers that used to hold ice cream or other foods. Eunice sets up a chair for me, and I sit between her and Amy, Sarah's four-year-old sister. Sarah and Amy eat thick sandwiches made of homemade bread, meat, and cheese. When Amy spills a little applesauce on her apron, Sarah immediately unbuttons it and helps Amy take it off so only her clean dress shows. She periodically brushes crumbs off Amy's dress, and when Amy dribbles more applesauce, Sarah just wipes it off without scolding her.

After dinner, we settle down to stitch again. I finally figure out how to use my thimble to push the needle through several stitches at a time.

What's the word for quilt in German?

Dorothy says something that sounds like "gvielt." When I ask how to spell that, the girls laugh merrily. Although they speak the Pennsylvania German dialect at home, when they write it's usually in English.

Often we fall silent and listen to the hum of women talking and laughing in low voices, the snap of needles being pulled through fabric, and the free play of preschoolers who troop through the room hugging Amish cloth dolls almost as big as they are. The children play in the back room most of the afternoon, but when they start throwing their dolls out the window, they have to run downstairs to pick them up again. Little Amy runs up to Sarah every hour or so and asks if it's time to go downstairs to the store. Sarah just smiles and whispers to her in German, and Amy scampers back to her friends.

We compare thimble fingers. Some girls' fingers have turned green, probably from their skin interacting with the metal of a thimble. Sarah shows us a hole in her thimble, worn through from so much use. "Sometimes the needle sticks through it and that's a surprise," she says.

About halfway through the afternoon, the women at the quilt behind us finish their last stitch. They unpin the edging and take it to another woman who spent the afternoon at the sewing machine by the window stitching children's clothing to send along with the quilts. She folds over the lining of the quilt to stitch down the binding, her feet working the treadle that propels the machine.

I take a break from stitching to watch Leona and her friend Alta set up a new quilt. One of the women pieced the top layer of the quilt at home, which means that she sewed small squares of fabric together to make one large design. Amish women usually use a treadle machine to piece all the squares together, and a lot of creativity and thought goes into choosing the fabric and planning the quilt.

The brightly colored patchwork tops a sandwich of layers. Underneath, Leona and Alta stretch an old blanket for warmth, then a sheet for backing. They pin these three layers together, stretch them over the frame, and clamp them in place. Then the hard work begins—the layers of fabric must be crisscrossed with tiny stitches to fasten them together and to make pockets of air to trap the warmth.

What is this design called? "A Trip around the World," says Leona. A fitting name for a quilt that will travel all the way to Haiti. A series of multicolored diamonds—yellow calico, blue, black, pink, beige, green—nestle inside the other, circling 'round and 'round the quilt, 'round and 'round the world.

For these charity quilts, the women either purchase discount bolts of fabric or cut up cast-off clothes from Goodwill, so the squares might be brightly colored gingham, calico, or some other design. For their quilts at home, the women use sewing scraps or the good parts of old clothes—thus plain, solid colors form their personal quilts.

I join the girls to stitch some more. As the afternoon wears on and we finish the outer edges, we roll up the ends to make the frame smaller. This way we can eventually reach the middle area without stretching. Soon we knock knees and bump heads as we hunch over the quilt.

Around 4:00 p.m., Sarah gathers up Amy and takes her downstairs for her long-awaited visit to the store.

When I leave at 4:15, fifteen women still bend over the frames. Before they finish this afternoon, there will be three more quilts ready to send to Haiti, an astonishing accomplishment. I wish I could see the faces of the people who receive these beautiful quilts so carefully stitched with laughter and love.

An Amish woman can express her creativity and add bright color to her home through quilting. Quilting styles vary in different Amish communities. Antique quilts from Lancaster, Pennsylvania, for instance, feature bold, dark, striking colors and geometric shapes.

Traditional Iowa Amish designs have wonderful names, such as Botch Handle, Hole in the Barn Door, and Sunshine and Shadow. Quilts called "samplers" include a combination of designs, such as Turkey Tracks, Log Cabin, Flying Geese, and variations of fan and star patterns.

Leona described a sampler quilt made by one family for their grandparents. It said, "God Bless Our Family, 45th Wedding Anniversary, John and Edna Mae 1946-1991," and included squares with the names of all their children and grandchildren stitched on them. Even the men and boys in the family sewed their own squares.

However skilled she eventually becomes at quiltmaking, an Amish girl will usually start with the simple Nine Patch design. Leona stitched her first Nine Patch quilt at age 12, and she's never quit since.

Here's how to start a Nine Patch quilt.

1. Cut five squares of the same color, each 1 1/2" by 1 1/2". Cut four more squares the same size but of a different color.
2. Using a sewing machine, sew the nine squares together, alternating the colors. (See Figure 2.)
3. These nine squares form the basic unit of the Nine Patch quilt. Make 16 of these Nine Patch squares.
4. Using plain fabric, cut 16 squares the same size as the Nine Patch squares.

5. Sew the Nine Patch squares and the plain squares together to create strips.

6. Sew the strips together, and you have pieced a Nine Patch quilt. The rest of the quilting process includes sewing on a border, stretching the Nine Patch quilt top on a quilting frame along with layers of filling and backing, and handstitching the layers together.

a nine patch and a nine patch quilt   figure 2

completed nine patch quilt

sample strip

a nine patch

Excerpts from *The Budget:*

Sept. 2—The past week has gone by without any rain. Has been foggy a bit in the morn. but soon turns out in the usual sunny, warm days.

The 4th son was added to the Evan and Ethel Gingerich home, born last eve. The 10 lb. boy was named Eric Jon. So Elrose, Eugene and Ernest have another bro. whose name starts with an E. Ernest and Esther Yoder and Mrs. Emma Gingerich are the grandparents.

Paul Helmuths' and Jeffrey Yoders' of Nappanee, Ind. arrived here Fri. eve. to spend the Labor Day weekend here with homefolks. Sharla Ropp also came along home, after having spent several weeks in Ind. working for her aunt.

Aug. 14—Ben Rabers' had a frolic to put an upstairs on the house they moved on their property. Sam Masts' have also been having frolics to get their house framed.

The Albany Hills schoolhouse was moved across the road last week.

Yesterday the girls and Ida Mae were here and we dressed 60 some fryers. In the evening the menfolk came and we grilled chicken and hamburgers and the rest got the ice cream in appreciation for all the free strawberries they got this spring.

chapter

9

a trip to Dorothy Mast's country store

*T*he Amish believe that life should
be spent in perfecting the spirit, not in pursuing material goods.
Amish children live far away from shopping malls, and they do not
even shop much in country stores.

The Amish families I met like to shop locally, buying from merchants in the Amish community. They strive to be self-sufficient and
try to make or grow everything that they need. Using styles and patterns passed down for generations, mothers and teenage girls sew all
the clothes for the family. Children wear hand-me-downs from older
brothers and sisters.

Amish parents may purchase certain toys—such as red wagons,
farm sets with plastic animals and buildings, and dolls. But many
preschool children play with homemade cloth Amish dolls with no
faces, to be completely plain.

Rather than accumulating material goods, the Amish teach their children to accumulate lifelong friendships, loving families, and the qualities of honesty, generosity, and selflessness.

From Amish wide-brimmed straw hats to fine china, the shelves at Dorothy Mast's Community Country Store burst with everything an Amish family doesn't make at home.

Even though it's only a few weeks before Christmas, my companions, Kathryn and Sharon Kauffman, ages 14 and six, are not thinking about Christmas shopping. Nor are they thinking about the gifts they will receive. In their Amish home, the birth of Christ is celebrated as a day for spiritual renewal, and presents are not emphasized.

"Usually, if we get a gift from our parents for our birthday, we won't get one for Christmas," says Kathryn.

Gifts are often homemade. One year for her mother's birthday, the whole family of 10 children drew a mural on a large piece of butcher paper. "The picture had a house with a garden, and Dad drew a dog digging in it," says Kathryn with a laugh. "That was to tease her, because she doesn't like it when our dog digs up her flowers."

Today Kathryn and Sharon wear matching light blue dresses. A black woven shawl protects Kathryn from the December wind; a black wool jacket shields Sharon. Both wear black Amish bonnets, black stockings, and sturdy black shoes shining with polish. Amish girls and women often dress this way when they go to town or to church.

As she gracefully glides slowly down the aisles of the store with her hands folded under her shawl, Kathryn's clear brown eyes reflect serenity and wisdom. Although she seems content to be silent, she speaks with confidence and usually ends her sentences with a pleasant smile or a laugh.

Sharon seems quite shy, speaking only when I talk to her. When I mention this to her mother later on, though, she laughs. It seems Sharon is quite the chatterbox at home.

Kathryn says she seldom goes to town, nor does she shop at Amish country stores like this one. Once a year, if she's outgrown her shoes (and if her older sister's hand-me-downs aren't in good shape), she comes to this store with her parents for the annual shoe and boot sale. When her parents leave their farm to shop a few times a month, they usually take one or two of the younger children in their horse and buggy. The older children, such as Kathryn, stay home to take care of the others.

The girls show me a few of the things their parents might purchase for the family: black stockings for the girls, suspenders for the boys, towels, sewing supplies, shoes, and boots. Kathryn points out the pink and blue knitted booties and bibs that her cousin makes for sale in the store and the caps that her grandmother knits.

As we pass the aisles of boots, shoes, and slippers, Kathryn laughs and describes the slippers she once crocheted. "I have to admit, they were pretty outlandish. They were all different colors, because I wanted to use up all our scraps of yarn."

In the toy department, Kathryn says, "This would be an ideal gift for a small Amish boy." She's pointing to a shiny miniature plow. For girls, the store sells dolls and baby bottles. I ask Sharon if she plays with a doll at home, and she smiles and nods. Kathryn says that her mother makes her younger sisters' dolls.

Do the children ever spend money of their own in town? "It's not likely," says Kathryn. "If we have any money of our own, our parents encourage us to save it and not to waste it on small things."

The prices are good, 89 cents for a ceramic mug that would cost $3.00 elsewhere. The kitchenware section includes large stainless steel mixing bowls, rolling pins, potato mashers, glassware—everything you'd need to set up a kitchen. Another shelf holds kerosene lamps and sturdy steel flat irons that heat on the stove.

"Girls my age sometimes exchange presents like this for our birthdays," says Kathryn, showing me some stationery with flowers on it. She usually likes to make her own gifts, such as a crocheted doily. "I like my presents to be useful and I like to make them myself."

Kathryn gets her love for making things from her mother, who draws illustrations for art teaching materials and Christian coloring books. She points to some colorful picture books of forest animals and says, "These are the kinds of books my mother would like, because she uses ideas from them for drawings of her own."

A bookshelf holds several Amish cookbooks, including one that Kathryn's family has at home. Another cookbook published locally, *Kalona Family Favorites,* includes a recipe by Kathryn's mother called the "No Recipe Cake."

"My mom put her easy made-up cake in here," Kathryn says. "Cooking is not something she really enjoys, so she likes this recipe because it's easy."

We stop next at Cedar Grove Fabrics. Like Dorothy Mast's, we find it on a country road beside a farm, but unlike Dorothy's, it doesn't serve many non-Amish customers. The new building contains rainbow rows of the solid-color fabrics that Amish women purchase to make their clothes. Kathryn shows me the kind of fabric she would use to make a Sunday dress (a fine, lightweight polyester in dark purple) and the plainer double knits that she'd use to make a school dress.

Kathryn likes green for her dresses. Does she select her own fabrics? "Usually Mom does, unless she decides that we may have a choice," she says, smiling. "But it must suit her."

The store even sells bolts of black woven wool, which Kathryn used to make the shawl she wears today. I asked her how she made the fringe.

"We just used scissors," she says with her wonderful laugh. "Some people make different kinds of fringe, but we like this fast kind."

I wonder if they make their own bonnets, too. Some families make their own, Kathryn says. "Mom finds them too time-consuming to make so she gets another Amish woman who has a talent to make ours."

Kathryn shows me an autograph book for sale in the store. "Most Amish girls own one," she says. "Our friends sign it, and if we go out of state and meet new people we ask them to sign it."

"Do you know what this is?" she asks. It's a wooden folding

clothes rack. Her family uses one to dry clothes when it rains outside. In winter, they hang the clothes out until they freeze dry and
then bring them inside to finish drying on the drying rack.

We're standing in front of a shelf holding dozens of wooden
plaques with Bible verses painted on them. Kathryn says, "These
are the kind of mottoes you might find in Amish homes. But our
family would not buy them, because we could make them ourselves.
They'd be less expensive and serve just as good a purpose."

On the way home I ask Kathryn if she will sing a song. She
sings a traditional Amish hymn, in German, that she learned in
church. Her voice weaves through the air like a golden thread, pure
and light. Almost like a Gregorian chant, Kathryn's voice stretches
long and slow, then up and down in many small notes. I feel a sense
of peace and a longing for divine perfection. A hawk floats above a
field nearby, the rise and dip of his wings matching the slow rhythm
of the song. The cows below join Kathryn's song, too, as we're all
drawn into a circle of beauty.

---

no recipe cake
contributed by Mrs. Norman Kauffman

1 part shortening
2 parts sugar
4 parts flour
1 tsp. baking powder to each cup flour
Eggs
Milk and flavoring

Variations: Use soda and sour milk combined. Add nuts,
raisins, chocolate chips, or chocolate powder.

A recipe to keep in your head.

From: *Kalona Family Favorites*. Compiled by Mrs.
Linda Hershberger. 1999 printing by G&R Publishing Co., 507 Industrial St., Waverly, IA 50677

part four

 customs

chapter

10

playing Dutch Blitz and Dare Base

*A*mish children don't watch TV,
and they don't play organized sports, join clubs, or take part in ex-
tra-curricular activities.

But that doesn't mean they don't have fun. Each fall when hay
bales fill the barn, children make tunnels in the hayloft, playing
harrowing games of tag. "We put mirrors at the corners, so we can
see someone coming and hide," one Amish boy told me. In the summer,
children swim and fish; in the winter they ice skate and sled. On Sunday afternoons, boys might go outside for a walk in the timber or play
croquet or lawn games, such as tag. The girls like to play Scrabble and
other board games.

Amish children and teenagers enjoy playing group sports, including baseball and volleyball, but they don't establish teams or
play for points. The Amish consider noncompetitiveness to be a

virtue and teach their children to cooperate rather than to compete. Similarly, the violent sports of boxing and football are not played by the Amish, because nonviolence is central to their faith. The only contact sport played by Amish boys is wrestling, although they don't wrestle at school.

At the same time, Amish children try their best at games. The children I met on school playgrounds didn't hold back from running fast and tagging me, an adult and a stranger. Cat and Mouse, a game where you clap a frying pan lid over a spool on a string before "the mouse" jerks it away, can get pretty wild at family gatherings, I'm told.

Singing is an important pastime for Amish people of all ages. Most families I visited sang in the morning after breakfast, at school, while doing the dishes, while milking the cows, or in the evening after supper. One Amish girl told me her older brother couldn't sing on key no matter how hard he tried, but other children I met sang with gusto and perfect pitch.

Without TV to pass the evening hours, many Amish children like to read, as do their parents. An Amish girl told me not to ask what time her family went to bed at night but to ask "some other respectable family." Reading, she said, was their downfall.

I t's recess at the Amish schoolhouse in Union Grove, North Carolina. The school building consists of two trailers the community bought from the local school district, one for grades one through four, the other for grades five to eight. Each trailer holds approximately 15 children.

I'm standing outside with Tom Coletti, the Amish teacher of the older students. Most of the older children play volleyball, with mixed teams of boys and girls. Light-hearted banter and laughter fills the air each time someone misses the ball or drops it.

Out on the green pasture beyond the sandy volleyball area, two first graders have tied their black bonnets on upside down to cover their eyes. They are being led by two friends.

"It's kind of a trust walk," says Tom, who sees me watching the blindfolded girls. The blindfolded girls walk fearlessly over hills and around trees, and finally all four crumple in a heap of laughter in the meadow.

"Me, play?" Tom responds to a smiling girl in glasses who just called out to him to play volleyball. "But the sides are exactly even," he says.

"The other team needs help," she points out. Tom tells me that the children love it when he plays, but today he stays put.

I watch several eight-year-old boys building a bridge with small wooden trestles in a sandbox. Just as they get it ready for their shiny metal trucks to drive over, another boy accidentally rolls over the bridge, knocking it down. I expect the bridge boys to do something, say something, but they just start building the bridge all over again.

"Nonresistance is instilled in Amish children at an early age," observes Tom. "Fighting is just not an option."

Later, after school, I drive to the Schrock home to talk to Verna, a slender girl of 13, and her 11-year-old brother, Johnny.

I enter the large two-story yellow house from the front porch. A long kitchen opens into a room where the family gathers often for singing after dinner (whenever someone gets a notion to sing and pulls out the books) and occasionally for board games such as Monopoly or checkers. Verna shows me how to play an Amish card game, Dutch Blitz. Each card displays a buggy, barrel, plow, or outdoor water pump. To play the game, you race to place all of your cards into different piles in a certain order.

The whole family recently played Dutch Blitz at a birthday party for their mother and eight-year-old Amos, born on the same day. "It got very loud and exciting," says Johnny. He says he doesn't like playing, because "you have to be so fast and my head gets a spinnin'."

What games do they like best? Verna says right now it's volleyball, although she says next week it might be softball. Johnny likes basketball best. There's a hoop inside their family's shop. A few nights ago, Johnny, his twin brothers, and two friends played a game in which each person tries to get 21 points, with difficult shots yielding higher points. They sometimes play basketball in teams, if enough boys show up. At school the children also like to play tag games called Circle Base and Dare Base, and when it's raining they play marbles indoors.

Verna's older sister Anna walks in holding Rachel, age four, still sleepy from her nap. Later, Rachel crosses the room to snuggle up to Verna, and I ask her what games she likes to play. She hides her face in Verna's lap.

Verna says, "Whenever I come home from school, Rachel begs me to jump on the trampoline with her." We walk outside to look at the trampoline, but Rachel doesn't want to jump on it now and scampers back inside.

While we're in the backyard, Verna, Johnny, and Amos show me how to play Circle Base and Dare Base. Amos chooses a pole of the wash line for a base, Verna takes a bush, and Johnny a tree. As far as I can understand, in Circle Base each player tries to capture the most bases by tagging other players whenever they leave their bases. Dare Base, I admit, is too complex for me, although Verna, Johnny, and Amos certainly understand the rules and enthusiastically chase each other until Johnny wins by capturing the other two.

On Sundays, after spending the morning at church, the family sometimes plays board games, such as Bible Trivia and Bible Challenge, or the children read Bible stories or take a walk. Often, another family joins them for Sunday dinner.

Like other Amish children, in their after-school hours Verna and Johnny do chores around the house. Verna helps her sisters and mother with canning or sewing, and Johnny helps in the family business by cutting and nailing shingles on storage sheds. It's time for him to be at work, so Johnny and I walk up the driveway to the shop where his father and brothers work. Johnny tells me that his 15-year-old twin brothers, Alvin and Abner, graduated from eighth grade and now spend their days learning their father's trade.

Buzzing saws, pounding hammers, and the smell of sawdust fill the roomy and tidy shop. The family produces the storage sheds in an assembly line, with one person cutting, two framing, two trimming and painting, and one roofing. Alvin moves with efficiency and skill, nailing white trim onto a blue shed. After asking permission from Leroy, their oldest brother and foreman, Alvin steps outside to talk to me.

We sit on a pile of cut lumber beside the driveway. Alvin is a serious youth who, along with his brother, already chose to be baptized and join the church.

How does he spend his weekends and evenings?

Besides playing an occasional game such as softball, basketball, or volleyball when he gets a chance, Alvin likes to ride the family's Standardbred horses. About once a month he goes camping with a group of friends.

"We don't go too far," he says. "We carry our tent and camping supplies into the woods. We just talk and tell stories around the campfire." Alvin says he belongs to a church group that visits older people to cheer them up with singing.

Why don't the Amish watch television?

"We feel that would be a detriment to our Christian life," explains Alvin. "At night after dinner I like to read. Mostly true stories, about the early Christians in Rome, or stories about dogs and horses, like *Wilderness Champion*."

Later I chat with Alvin's twin brother, Abner, who is as smiling as Abner is serious. Blond bangs frame his face. "Each person in the family has different interests," he says. His is the outdoors. He often walks in the woods, sometimes with his brother or a friend, sometimes by himself.

How long does he stay out? "Oh, anywhere from 15 minutes to two hours."

He sometimes just goes into the woods and sits. "I'm learning about the animals, teaching myself," he says. "I've got a couple of places where I usually go to see deer." Other wildlife he tracks are fox and birds.

While the twins mix freely with girls their age in games and social events, they won't start dating until age 18. When they turn 16, they will be given their own horse and buggy and join a youth group, which meets for singing every other Sunday night. Other favorite pastimes for teenagers in this Amish community include taffy pulls, roller skating, ice skating, and swimming.

Before I leave, I ask Verna and Johnny if they ever run out of fun things to do. "Oh no!" they say in unison, their smiles telling it all.

how to play dollar up

Dollar Up is a game Johnny Schrock likes to play at school. One person bats and the others field balls. If a fielder catches a ball on three bounces, it counts as 25 cents. Two bounces = 50 cents, one bounce = 75 cents, and a fly = $1.00. The first fielder to earn $3.00 in points gets to bat next.

marbles

While the boys play Dollar Up, the girls might play marbles (although boys, too, play marbles indoors in rainy weather). To play: Draw a chalk circle about three feet in diameter on the ground or cement floor. In the center of this circle, draw a smaller circle only one foot in diameter. Place all the marbles (except the large "shooter" marble) inside the small circle. Then place the shooter marble outside the large circle and flick it toward the other marbles. The object is to shoot as many marbles as possible outside the large circle.

Verna says that you can count one point for each marble, or you can count two points for the solid-colored ones and one point for the others.

chapter

11

courtship and marriage

*A*fter joining the church, Amish young people start dating, usually around the age of 18. Young people meet at Sunday evening "singings" held in houses or barns after church services. A young man may take a girl home from a Sunday singing, and he may sit in the parlor with her. The rest of the family pretends not to notice the courtship, although younger brothers might tease the young man.

Marriages are not prearranged by the parents; they remain a matter of choice by the couple. The couple and their parents keep the engagement secret until the couple gets "published," which means the bishop announces at Sunday services that the wedding will take place the following week. Others may enjoy looking for clues, such as the bride's family growing more celery or raising extra chickens.

Weddings are the most festive occasions in Amish life. In some communities they take place in the fall after harvest, since then everyone can relax. The family and friends prepare a huge sit-down feast for 200 or more people, which takes place after a solemn but simple three-hour ceremony. The festivities go on all day, with children playing lawn games, adults socializing, and everyone singing. In the evening, another meal is served. For both meals, friends take charge of the serving, cooking, and cleaning up so the bride's parents can enjoy the wedding day.

The Amish couple does not take a honeymoon as we know it, but in some communities, after a few weeks at home, they usually visit relatives or go on a sightseeing trip. Most couples today plan ahead and rent a place of their own after the wedding.

Marriage for the Amish is a commitment that lasts throughout life; divorce is not an option if a person wants to stay Amish. Most Amish couples start their families right away. And with lots of practice helping at home and on the farm, the young couple feels confident they can raise their own family in the Amish way of life.

I almost don't recognize the Yoder farm when I drive up, but fortunately Nancy, her arms loaded with clothes from the clothesline, greets me. Baby Wayne, now a young boy of five, stands by the door. I realize it has been nearly four years since I've visited.

Nancy spent the last week at home caring for Robert, now 13, whose appendix ruptured. He sits in a chair in the living room doing his schoolwork while we chat. A quilting frame is stored along one wall, used by Nancy to stitch custom quilts.

"When Robert got to the hospital, one of our neighbors, who is a nurse, was working on his floor," says Nancy. "I thought that was really nice."

I get caught up on all the children. Annie is now 23 and married. Regina, 21, works at an Amish country store and at the Amish school as a teacher's assistant. Today she's traveling to Illinois with her boyfriend and his parents.

"Do you remember me?" asks a slender young woman walking down the stairs. It takes me a moment to recognize Grace, who is now 17. She folds laundry while Nancy and I talk. Grace started attending young people's gatherings last year. In a few months, she'll start taking instruction for joining the church.

"In this community, the children start going to young folk's gatherings at 16," says Nancy. "But they don't start dating until 18. They usually join the Amish church before starting to date."

What do the young people do at the gatherings?

"On the Sundays when we have church, the young folks have their singings in the evening," says Nancy. "They have supper together and then refreshments or a snack later on. After supper they sing gospel songs. Half are in English, and half are in German. If we don't do it half and half, the young people might forget to learn the German ones."

Usually a first date for an Amish couple consists of the boy asking to drive a girl home from the singing in his buggy.

"Through the week there might also be a gathering—just every now and then—whenever anybody wants to do something," adds Grace.

"The young people may play volleyball games in summer, and in the winter, go ice skating," says Nancy. There might be special gatherings for harvesting nuts or stacking wood.

Parents chaperone the gatherings. "Like if Toby and I invited the young people for a taffy pull, we'd be there with them," says Nancy. "Then in the evening they'd play games in the living room."

Grace says that her group plays such games as Congress or Catch Phrase, a word game you can buy at Wal-Mart. Card games, such as Skippo, U-No, and Dutch Blitz, are also favorites.

In Amish society, young folks choose their own marriage partners. "To begin with, the church asks the boys and girls who are dating age to pray to the Lord who their partner should be," says Nancy. "As long as he's attending church in good standing, we let our daughters choose. We don't try to make it our business. Oh, sometimes a boy has had to settle down a bit before the parents would let him date their daughter. That has happened." She smiles.

"If a boy asks a girl and the girl is not interested at all, she politely says 'no.'" Nancy says. "That happens. Lots of times a boy has an eye on a girl before he asks for a date. Often she knows and expects him to ask."

I can see that Nancy feels restless, with nothing to do with her hands. I'm not surprised, then, when she calls Wayne, who pushes a toy truck along an imaginary road on the living room floor. "Ask Grace for the white shirt you wore last Sunday," she says to him. "I want to change the sleeves." He brings it to her. "Let me measure on your arm. She holds the white shirtsleeve up to his arm.

The shirt is one that Robert wore. "Most of his clothes are hand-me-downs from Robert," says Nancy. She starts removing the stitches on the cuff.

"And I got a lot of hand-me-downs from David," adds Robert, who is working on schoolwork now. He peers out the window at David driving by in the pony cart to pick up Leah at school.

Will Robert be going back to school soon? "They said I can if I want to." He smiles, enjoying having the choice. "If I'm at home, I'd rather work outside and not sit in the house and do schoolwork. I can help chore now. Can lift 20 pounds. When I first came home I could only lift five."

Leah, now nine, walks in with a big smile. She nods when her mother asks if she remembers me. "Usually Robert drives her from school," says Nancy. "She's too small yet to drive a horse." Leah goes upstairs to change from her school dress, then settles on the end of the couch with a book. Later, she carries in firewood, her main chore after school.

Nancy never dated anyone steadily except Toby. Was she thinking about him before he asked her?

"Afterwards I thought I had been, but at the time I felt surprised," she says. "I knew him before, but just kind of saw him around. I didn't know his ways until after I started dating. He always liked horses—it wasn't long before I figured that out. But I didn't mind that because I loved horses, too."

Nancy and Toby dated two and a half years. During that time

they saw each other at least once a week, sometimes twice, but hardly ever more than that.

What does an Amish couple look for in each other? "Even though we have the same religion and lifestyle, it's possible we might not agree on some things," says Nancy. "When you're dating you want to know: Do you like each other? Would he be a good father? Do you have a happy time and is there a good feeling when you're together?"

With four of their seven daughters married, Nancy and Toby are used to putting on weddings. Nancy says with a laugh, "After Annie's wedding, Toby said, 'Well, we're over halfway with the weddings.'"

Nancy says in their community, young people get married throughout the year, not just in the fall. "Our daughters can't marry except in the spring or summer! We don't have enough room inside." For their first daughter's wedding, they built a large metal shed in the back. That's where they hold all their wedding meals and also church when it's their turn to host the service.

The Yoders invited 250 guests to Annie's wedding. The service took place at a neighbor's house, then everyone arrived at the bride's home for the noon meal.

"At weddings 20 to 25 ladies help the bride's mother cook the meal, and they call them the chief cooks," says Nancy. "All I do that day is walk around and tell them what to do. But oh! Your head just about spins. There may be six or seven ladies to peel potatoes, usually 100 pounds, and they make that into mashed potatoes. Four or five ladies do the meat. I have to tell them how I want it cooked. There's a lot of seeing after, that's for sure."

Nancy, who married at age 19, talks easily about her marriage. "I was plenty young. We were married in '68 and had our first daughter one year and three months later. Of course, I was ready for a baby by then."

She says that yes, an Amish wife is supposed to be obedient to her husband, and he definitely is the head of the household. But she also says, "Toby and I like to be more equal when we make decisions. If the husband is like most of them, he will get his wife's say and see what she thinks before making a decision." She says her husband is her friend and the "pillar of the farm."

The Amish value harmony in family life above all. "We just learn from young up that when you marry, it's for life. I think if you live close to God and trust in God it all works together. Building up the community, being a good influence to everyone and especially to the younger generation is important."

What is the major challenge to Amish marriages? That stumps Nancy for a while. "If the husband and wife are obedient like they should be and have God with them in their home, there shouldn't be any problems. I just don't know what the problem would be."

She herself couldn't remember any major challenges in her own marriage. Later, as if she's been thinking about that question, she says, "There have been little things, like when the children were young and I needed more drawer space. But he was so busy and didn't want to stop his work on the farm to go find a dresser. I remember that kind of upset me. Later we did buy a couple of used dressers. I guess you just kind of have to wait until the time is right. We are taught to be patient—and that goes a long way."

She's been married 31 years. "We've had some conflicts but they weren't so big that we couldn't talk them over. That's the main thing. If you did say things you shouldn't have, you can say you're sorry and ask for forgiveness. That goes a long way."

Is it true that Amish parents try not to argue in front of the children? "I respect the ones who don't argue," she says with a smile. "But sometimes things have to be said now whether the children are there or not." She also says that it's important to talk things over in marriage and to "be careful it doesn't become a big issue."

We decide to go visit Annie. Like Nancy's other married children, Annie lives close by.

"We're just human, that's just it," says Nancy as she ties on her black outside bonnet. "Only we have more rules to live by than other people, and we try to live by those rules with God's help. God is really the head of the household."

Before we leave, I ask to see the quilt Nancy started for Regina. It's on a quilting frame in the basement. "Regina did the piecing herself," she says. It's a spectacular design, called the Colonial Star, and the colors are bold and dramatic—burgundy, black, and pink. I remember seeing Regina crochet an afghan, called Spanish Lace, on one of my earlier visits. It also was black and burgundy.

"Yes, these are her favorite colors," says Nancy. Nancy is completing the endless tiny stitches in designs of flowers and swirls all over the quilt.

Nancy says she gives each of her children three quilts when they leave home. "My mother gave me three, and Toby's mother gave him three, so we were well covered with bed quilts!"

I drive the few miles to Annie and Lester's. "Lester wants to buy a farm, but nothing has come up yet," says Nancy as we drive up to Annie's trailer. "In the meantime, they rent this small farm. Lester works out as a carpenter, but he still plans to plow for crops this spring."

Annie's brother, Dan, lives across the street with his wife and baby on their own 40-acre farm. Right now they live in a trailer but plan to build their house soon. Dan married Lester's sister, Betty, so the two couples are close. They married just a few months apart.

Nancy says that if Annie were home she'd be at the window. So we drive down the street to the store where Annie works shelving groceries. "Annie said she just didn't have enough to do at home," says Nancy. "She always was one who liked to be busy."

Today Annie works behind the counter taking Regina's place while she is away. She talks and jokes easily with the Amish customers, displaying the same merry laugh that I remember from my first visit so many years ago. At one point Annie tears off the receipt she just wrote and throws it in the wastebasket. "You can see I am no Regina!" she says with a laugh.

Nancy and I cruise the shelves while Annie waits on customers. Mantles, lanterns, hats, boots, and kitchenware fill the store. I hold up a flowered china bowl. Is this the kind of gift someone would give a newly married Amish couple, I ask?

"Yes, and these too," says Nancy. She points to a set of plastic bowls and plates. Kitchenware and farm tools are favorite gifts from friends. A group of young men might get together and buy a wheelbarrow or handyman jack to lift heavy loads.

Family and friends also give the young couple a grocery shower, so they have everything they need to eat for a few weeks.

Parents give much bigger gifts. Besides the three quilts, Nancy and Toby give their daughters a bed from home, a new wooden dresser, and a cow. The sons receive a bed, a secretary (wooden roll-top desk), and a horse. The spouse's parents also give big items to help the young couple get started.

Nancy says that most couples have collected the furniture they need by the time they set up housekeeping. Because of the high cost of farmland, today's young couples face a much harder time acquiring a farm than when she and Toby started out.

"It helps if the boy can borrow money from his dad," she says. "Then he can take the time he needs to pay back the loan at low or no interest. We did that." On the other hand, her daughter Ruby and her husband took out an FHA loan to buy their farm, and making the payments was hard. Nancy says Ruby didn't have a penny to spare.

"Some of the older boys advised Dan to work a few years and set money aside for the down payment before getting married. Both Dan and Lester were able to do that."

In between customers, we chat with Annie, who will be going straight to the barn to chore when she gets off work. She says she can't remember when she first met Lester. He lived across the field and went to the same church but to a different school. "I just knew him. We had our first date the same evening as Dan and Betty. But I noticed him before that." She also knew his parents.

Did she want him to ask her on a date? "Oh yes," she says with a quick smile. But she didn't talk about it. "You don't want other people to know who you like, other than your closest friend."

They dated for three years before they married. Were they in love? "I would say it would really be more like a quiet, deep love and friendship," says Annie. "It's not like romance books."

"Oh, but you did go around with stars in your eyes and your head in the clouds," remembers Nancy. "I sometimes had to remind you to get back to earth."

When he asked her to marry him, "it was no shock," she says. "He would sometimes say, 'If I were married I would. ...' We talked it over."

"But he had to ask the question sometime," adds Nancy.

Although they didn't call it a honeymoon, Annie and her husband took a train trip out West after their marriage. Two other couples accompanied them: Dan and his wife Betty, along with Annie's older sister Darla and her husband.

"Oh yes," says Annie when I ask if her husband is her best friend. A sparkling smile flashes across her face. "And I sure wouldn't want to be single again."

So far, she foresees no difficulties in her marriage. "Not if we both do our part," Annie says with great conviction, "which is just trying to keep each other happy and not to ever, ever want to start arguing."

She says that her husband is very considerate and that "you just try to agree with each other."

Would married friends talk to each other about everyday problems? "Oh I think so," says Nancy. "If the sisters are real good friends I think they discuss things. I and mine do, anyway."

Annie says she's never heard of any need for marriage counseling in the community. What would a couple having trouble do? "Talk to the minister," says Annie.

I wonder aloud if Amish marriages are more harmonious because from childhood on people are taught to serve others, rather than thinking about what *I* want, what *I* need.

"Everybody has that tendency," says Nancy. "In church we are taught that everybody must try not to think about themselves but to think about others."

"And if you think about others first it goes better," says Annie.

"It's the way we are raised," says Nancy. "So we don't know any different. Just like we don't miss TV, we don't miss the things we've never had."

Excerpts from *The Budget:*

BONDUEL, WI

Oct. 15—A beautiful autumn day with temperature in the 70s. Sun. was another such day. The young folks got together at Jerry Lee Yoders' and the boys went horseback riding and the girls had a picnic.

Early Mon. morning Mrs. (Melvin) Katie Miller and children, Allen Bontragers' and Lester Bontragers' left for Wayne Co., Ohio, where they plan to attend the wedding on Thurs. of Allen, son of Albert Yoders', and Verna Mast. They will be gone most of the week. Melvin stayed home to take care of chores, etc.

This morning Mose Gingerich left for Milton, Ia., to attend a wedding at Noah Hostetlers'. Harry J. Bontrager went along to visit at his son Ora's.

HAVEN, KS

Aug. 13—Pleasant weather. Had over 2" rain on Sat. morn.

Ernest Eashes took out some walls some time ago, creating a big dining room. The extra seating space was sure needed Sun. when many visitors joined us for the baptismal services for Weldon Headings and Anna Bontrager.

Weldon and Anna were also published to be married, on Sept. 5. He is son of Mervin and Treva Headings and her parents are Jonas and Irene Bontrager.

It doesn't happen too often that the 3 oldest children all get married within 2 mos. time, but for Mervin and Treva, twill be so. Weldon's will be first and then son Stan and girlfriend Lori Kough on Sept. 28, and dau. Colleen and Steven Yoder on Oct. 24, so if Mervin and Treva sprout a few extra gray hairs this fall, we'll understand.

further reading

Bender, Sue. *Plain and Simple: A Woman's Journey to the Amish.* New York: HarperCollins, 1990.

Bial, Raymond. *Amish Home.* Boston: Houghton Mifflin Company, 1993.

Bishop, Robert, and Elizabeth Safanda. *A Gallery of Amish Quilts: Design Diversity from a Plain People.* New York: Dutton, 1976.

Braun, Anneliese. *Angelus Silesius, The Cherubinic Pilgrim: A Perennial Calendar, Selected and Translated from the Sayings of Anneliese Braun.* Nienburg: Hannemann Verlag, 1985.

Erb, Jean. "Amish Farmers Plow Ahead Despite Tough Times in Iowa." *The Des Moines Register,* 25 August 1985, p. 1A.

Gingerich, Melvin. *The Mennonites in Iowa.* Iowa City: State Historical Society of Iowa, 1939.

Good, Merle, and Phyllis Good. *Twenty Most Asked Questions about the Amish and Mennonites.* Lancaster, Pa.: Good Books, 1979.

Haders, Phyllis. *Sunshine and Shadow: The Amish and Their Quilts.* Pittstown, N.J.: The Main Street Press, 1976.

Holstein, Jonathan. *The Pieced Quilt: An American Design Tradition.* New York: Galahad Books, 1973.

Horton, Roberta. *An Amish Adventure: A Workbook for Color in Quilts.* Lafayette, Calif.: C&T Publishing, 1983.

Hostetler, John A. *Amish Society,* Fourth Edition. Baltimore: Johns Hopkins University Press, 1993.

Hostetler, John A., and Gertrude Enders Huntington. *Children in Amish Society: Socialization and Community Education.* Fort Worth, Ind.: Holt, Rinehart and Winston, Inc., 1971.

Israel, Fred. *Meet the Amish.* New York: Chelsea House Publishers, 1986.

Kraybill, Donald B.; photographs by Lucian Niemeyer. *The Old Order Amish: Their Enduring Way of Life.* Baltimore: The Johns Hopkins University Press, 1993.

Kraybill, Donald B. *The Riddle of Amish Culture.* Baltimore: The

Johns Hopkins University Press, 1989.

McGrath, William R. *Amish Folk Remedies for Plain and Fancy Ailments.* Burr Oak, Mich.: Chupp's Books, 1985.

Meyer, Carolyn. *Amish People: Plain Living in a Complex World.* New York: Atheneum. 1976.

Pellman, Rachel T. *Amish Quilt Patterns.* Intercourse, Pa.: Good Books, 1984.

Pellman, Rachel, and Kenneth Pellman. *Amish Crib Quilts.* Intercourse, Pa.: Good Books, 1984.

Schreiber, William I. *Our Amish Neighbors.* Chicago: The University of Chicago Press, 1962.

Schwieder, Elmer, and Dorothy Schwieder. *A Peculiar People: Iowa's Old Order Amish.* Ames: Iowa State University Press, 1975.

Schwieder, Elmer, and Dorothy Schwieder. *Patterns and Perspectives in Iowa History.* Ames: Iowa State University Press, 1973.

Scott, Stephen. *Why Do They Dress That Way?* Intercourse, Pa.: Good Books, 1986.

Scott, Stephen. *Plain Buggies: Amish, Mennonite, and Brethren Horse-Drawn Transportation.* Lancaster, Pa.: Good Books, 1981.

Stewart, Jillian. *Amish Cooking.* Philadelphia: Courage Books, 1995.

Swander, Mary. *Out of This World: A Woman's Life among the Amish.* New York: Penguin Books, 1995.

Wagler, David L. *Stories behind the News.* Bloomfield, Iowa: David L. Wagler, 1993.

Warner, James A., and Donald M. Denlinger. *The Gentle People: A Portrait of the Amish.* Soudersburg, Pa.: Mill Bridge Museum, 1969.

Weaver, Sarah M. *Over One Hundred of Grandma's Home Remedies: The Plain People's Method on How to Cut Down on Doctor Bills.* Millersburg, Ohio: Fani's Books, 1992.

Wittmer, Joe. *The Gentle People: Personal Reflections of Amish Life.* Minneapolis: Educational Media corporation, 1991.

Yoder, Joseph W. *Rosanna of the Amish.* Scottsdale: Herald Press, 1973.

Zielinski, John M. *The Amish across America.* Grinnell: Iowa Heritage Galleries, 1983.